BRILLIANT
BREADMAKING
IN YOUR
BREAD MACHINE

BRILLIANT
BREADMAKING
IN YOUR
BREAD MACHINE

Catherine Atkinson

A How To Book

ROBINSON

ROBINSON

First published in Great Britain in 2013 Spring Hill,
an imprint of How To Books Ltd

This edition published in 2015 by Robinson

Text © Catherine Atkinson 2013

1 3 5 7 9 10 8 6 4 2

A CIP catalogue record for this book is available from the British Library.

ISBN: 978-1-90586-295-5

Produced for How To Books by Deer Park Productions, Tavistock, Devon
Designed and typeset by Mousemat Design Ltd
Edited by Wendy Hobson
Printed and bound in Great Britain by Bell & Bain Ltd, Glasgow

Robinson
An imprint of
Little, Brown Book Group
Carmelite House
50 Victoria Embankment
London EC4Y 0DZ

An Hachette UK Company
www.hachette.co.uk

www.littlebrown.co.uk

NOTE: The material contained in this book is set out in good faith for general
guidance and no liability can be accepted for loss or expense incurred as a result of
relying in particular circumstances on statements made in the book. Laws and
regulations are complex and liable to change, and readers should check the current
position with relevant authorities before making personal arrangements.

How To Books are published by Robinson, an imprint of Little, Brown Book Group.
We welcome proposals from authors who have first-hand experience of their subjects.
Please set out the aims of your book, its target market and its suggested contents in an
email to Nikki.Read@howtobooks.co.uk

Contents

Online Information and Suppliers

The author and publisher would like to thank the following companies who lent equipment for testing or provided flours and bread-making ingredients.

Kenwood
www.kenwoodworld.com

Morphy Richards
www.morphyrichards.co.uk

Lakeland Limited
Alexandra Buildings, Windermere, Cumbria, CA23 1BQ • 01539 488100 •
www.lakelandlimited.com
A wide range of bread-making equipment, including bread machines, bread mixes, bread storage bags and boxes. Available by mail order online and from their many shops.

Doves Farm
Salisbury Road, Hungerford, Berkshire, RG17 0RF • 01488 684880 •
www.dovesfarm.co.uk
A huge range of flours and bread making ingredients, all available by mail order. Organic flour and gluten-free specialists.

Claybrooke Mill
Claybrooke Magna, Lutterworth, Leicestershire, LE17 5DB • 01455 202443 •
www.claybrookewatermill.co.uk
Many organic and non organic and stoneground flours, including French flour, unusual blends and mixes and other bread making ingredients. Mail order available.

Introduction

Nothing beats the wonderful aroma of freshly baked bread, but in today's busy society few of us have the time to make it from scratch. Now all the laborious mixing, kneading, proving and baking can be done by your bread machine. All you need to do is to weigh out a few simple ingredients and let the machine do the work, creating loaves with maximum flavour and minimum fuss.

The benefits of home-baked bread are obvious. Not only do you get warm and fresh bread from your machine, you know exactly what's in it – no additives or preservatives, only wholesome ingredients in a loaf created to suit your personal preferences. With over 100 recipes to choose from, there are plenty of breads here that you won't find on every supermarket shelf, from the simplest farmhouse white and traditional wholemeal loaf to speciality breads made with flours such as spelt and rye and all manner of flavoured breads; the only limit is your imagination! Whether you're searching for a healthy brunch or lunchbox bread, sweet tea-time treat, or must-have dinner party accompaniment, you'll find something to suit in the following chapters.

This book takes you through the basic techniques and demystifies all that is essential to making good bread. A comprehensive introduction provides advice on different settings and programmes. Troubleshooting questions and answers will guide you through bread-making dilemmas to help you get perfect results every time.

Most of the recipes in the following chapters have three sets of ingredients, allowing you to make an average medium-sized loaf or, if you prefer, you can bake a larger loaf or a small one in a compact bread machine. Whichever type, flavour or size of loaf you choose, those you bake yourself will be infinitely more satisfying than bought baked bread.

CHAPTER 1

Bread Machine Basics

Bread machines take all the hard work out of making bread. Your machine will mix and knead the dough and ensure that it rises and bakes at the right temperature. To make most of the breads in this book, all you need to do is add the ingredients in the right order, decide the colour of the crust and press the start button. In just a few hours you will have a perfectly baked loaf.

Buying a bread machine
Like most kitchen appliances, there are many different bread-making machines to choose from. They all work on the same basic principles, and current models all have a white bread, wholewheat, dough and rapid setting. Less expensive machines tend to have fewer programmes compared with those that may cost two or three times as much, so as well as price and appearance, you need to decide which features you would find essential or useful, such as extra settings for gluten-free bread, cake-baking or jam-making. If you want to make a lot of breads with seeds, nuts or dried fruits, you may find an automatic dispenser handy, and if you can't resist peeking at your loaf while it rises and bakes, a viewing window is a must.

One of the most important factors to consider is the size and shape of the finished loaf, which is determined by the bread pan. Bread machine loaf sizes can vary from 450g to a massive 1.5kg, although most machines have no more than three loaf-size settings: small (450–500g), medium or standard (750–800g) and large (900g–1kg).

The majority of the recipes in this book are geared towards making a standard 750g loaf, but most also give quantities of ingredients needed for a larger 900g–1kg and a small 375–500g (compact size) as well.

Most people opt for a medium-sized machine, and these tend to have a tall, slightly square bread pan. Loaves cooked in these machines can be turned on their side for slicing into square slices. For these machines, simply follow the quantities of ingredients listed first, although you should also be able to make a larger or smaller loaf, if you prefer. Larger machines tend to make a rectangular loaf, like traditional farmhouse bread. In these machines, it is best to follow the standard or large set of ingredients. You can make a small loaf in a large machine but it will be shaped like a classic loaf in length and width, but only half the height, which is not quite so successful. Compact bread machines will only make a small loaf (although you can, of course, make more loaves when you are catering for a lot of people!) For these machines, you should use the quantities given for small loaves, as these are specially designed for these small machines.

For some machines, you can also buy a round bread pan as an additional extra, which are fantastic for making traditional milk bread and speciality loaves such as panettone.

A bread machine takes up a fair amount of room, so choose a machine that you can either store easily or that fits the space you have available. If you are planning to keep it on a kitchen surface and aesthetics are important, you may also want to choose something that fits into the style of your kitchen and matches your other appliances. Many models are available in white, black or stainless steel. You should also think about the height of the machine if you plan to position it under low kitchen cupboards, as you will need sufficient room to lift the lid and comfortably remove the bread after baking.

Running costs may be a further consideration, especially if part of your reason for buying a bread machine is to reduce your grocery bills. Although a machine-baked loaf will cost you about the same price as cheap, white, sliced supermarket bread, you can create good-quality bakery and deli-type breads at a fraction of the price. Bread machines consume little energy; the standard programme uses about 0.34KWh of electricity – around the same amount as boiling 3 litres of water in an average kettle, but consumption varies slightly between different models.

It is also worth checking out online reviews for the particular model you are interested in before you buy. These can often give you an insight as to the reliability of the machine, whether there is a good after-sales support system and whether it is relatively simple to get additional or replacement items such as bread pans. It will also let you know about any 'niggles' that current owners have, such as noisy motors, or viewing windows which steam up so that you cannot see into the machine.

Safety features
Some breadmakers include a power-failure mechanism so that if you inadvertently turn off the power socket or if there is a short power cut, the programme will resume as soon as

power is restored. This is usually limited to between 10 and 30 minutes and shouldn't affect the bread too much if it occurs during the kneading or proving cycle, but if power is cut for more than 10 minutes during the baking cycle you may have to discard the part-baked loaf and start again.

Your machine may also have an overload protection device that will stop the motor if the kneading blade is restricted, for example if the bread dough is very hard. This stops the machine and will automatically re-start it in about 30 minutes, so you have plenty of time to solve the problem.

Using the delay timer

For many, waking up to freshly baked bread is one of the great advantages of owning a bread machine. Simply put all the ingredients into the bread machine before you go to bed or out for the day and set the timer, so that the bread is ready at a time that suits you. If you want a machine that you can use overnight, check that that it doesn't have a loud bleeper that sounds part-way through the kneading cycle – the purpose of the alarm is to remind you to add extra ingredients such as seeds and nuts, but you won't appreciate that at 3.30 a.m! When you are using the timer, do not add perishable ingredients such as eggs or milk (you can add skimmed milk powder instead – see page 24).

Choosing the right bread programmes

The recipes in this book have been tested in a variety of bread machines from different manufacturers and should suit all machines, but you should always read through the instruction manual which comes with your model, as programmes do vary from machine to machine and a few may require ingredients to be added in a different order to that given here. It's important to choose the right programme to produce a perfect loaf of bread as the lengths of kneading, rising and baking times vary to suit the type of flour and other ingredients that you are using.

Most machines have a preheating cycle built in on most programmes either prior to mixing or during the kneading phase, so you use ingredients straight from the fridge. Many also have a keep-warm facility, which will circulate hot air for a further 30–60 minutes when the loaf has finished baking.

Basic or normal white: The most commonly used programme, this is ideal for white loaves and mixed grain or soft-grain loaves where strong white bread flour is the main ingredient. It is also used for many flavoured and enriched breads. On some machines this may be referred to as a the 'premium bread' programme. It takes 3–4 hours.

Wholewheat: This programme is longer and may have up to 3 risings because wholemeal, brown rye and Granary breads tend to be heavier and the bran in the flour retards yeast activity. There is normally a preheat time as well, to speed up yeast action and to allow the bran to soak up liquid when the dough mixes. It takes $3\frac{1}{2}$–$4\frac{1}{4}$ hours.

Rapid, fastbake or eco: An accelerated programme that takes a much shorter time, this is usually complete in 1–$1\frac{1}{2}$ hours. Some machines have several rapid cycles for white and wholewheat breads. The finished bread won't be quite as even-textured or as well risen as a loaf cooked on a normal cycle and recipes usually contain a little more yeast and start with warm rather than cold liquid. Many of the simpler breads in this book can be cooked on this cycle, but you should avoid those with a high proportion of wholemeal, brown or rye flour. If your machine doesn't have a special gluten-free bread programme, you can use this cycle for gluten-free bread mixes, which don't require long mixing or rising times.

French: For loaves that contain little or no fat or sugar, this setting gives bread a crisper crust and airy, open texture. It has a longer rising cycle and is ideal for use with Type 55 French flour or unbleached white flour. It takes $3\frac{3}{4}$–4 hours.

Sandwich: For soft bread with thick, soft crusts which, as the name suggests, are ideal for sandwich making, this cycle takes 3–$3\frac{1}{4}$ hours.

Sweet or brioche: For rich breads with a high fat and/or sugar content, this has a longer kneading and rising programme to cope with the extra ingredients and ensure that the crust doesn't over-brown. These are sometimes two separate programmes, with the brioche setting being for the very richest loaves and the sweet programme being slighter shorter. It takes $3\frac{3}{4}$–$4\frac{1}{4}$ hours.

Cake programme: This cycle mixes the ingredients and bakes non-yeasted mixtures, such as teabreads and cakes. This is only available on a few machines; many just have the 'bake' programme. It takes around $1\frac{1}{4}$ hours.

Bake only: If your machine has this cycle, it enables you to bake teabreads and cakes such as gingerbread. As the breadmaker doesn't preheat before baking starts, this isn't suitable for sponges and similar cakes which need to go in a hot oven. It takes around 1 hour.

Extra bake: Often featured on smaller, compact bread machines, this is similar to the 'bake only' programme for making cakes. It can also be used to extend cooking time when another selected programme has finished, for example if you decide you want a darker crust on bread.

Dough: This cycle mixes, kneads and proves dough ready for shaping and baking in a conventional oven. Some machines differentiate between types of dough and have individual programmes for white bread dough, wholewheat dough and pizza dough.

Other programmes
There are a few more unusual programmes and features on the most expensive machines. As only a few machines have these, there are no recipes in this book using these settings, so you should consult your instruction manual for guidance.

Jam: Fruit and sugar are added to the bread pan then, when the cycle is complete, the jam can be spooned into sterilised jars and sealed as you would for conventionally made jam.

Pasta: This mixes and kneads pasta dough ready for rolling and shaping.

Butter: Some machines even have a 'churn' setting which will agitate cream without heat to make butter.

Sizes
The weight of the finished loaves will obviously vary but, in general, most recipes are for a standard (or medium) 750g loaf, although sometimes additional ingredients make this up to 850g.
Where appropriate, I have also given ingredients quantities for a large (900g) loaf, which should be baked on the 1kg programme, and a small (450–500g) loaf, which should be baked on the 500g programme. As mentioned above, the small loaf is most suitable for compact bread machines and not as successful in large machines.

Twelve simple steps to the perfect loaf

1 Before you start: Stand the bread machine on a work surface, unplugged and with plenty of space around it for air to circulate. Lift up the lid and remove the bread pan by holding both sides of the handle and pulling upwards or gently wiggling and twisting, depending on the bread machine. Fit the kneading blade on the shaft; it should only fit in one position as the hole in the blade and the shaft are D-shaped (if you are unsure, check your manual). If the blade is collapsible (i.e. folds down at the end of kneading time), make sure that it is vertical at this stage.

2 Add the liquid: Pour the water, milk or other liquid into the bread pan, unless the instructions for your machine tell you to add the dry ingredients first (in which case reverse the order of ingredients in the recipes in this book). If you are adding sticky liquid ingredients, such as malt extract or golden syrup, stir them into the liquid before pouring into the pan.

3 Enrich the mixture: To ensure that bread keeps for longer and to add to its flavour and moistness, fat such as oil or butter are added. If you prefer a solid fat such as butter or margarine, make sure it is soft and preferably at room temperature so that it mixes easily; if it is slightly hard, cut it into small pieces or gently melt before adding. You can also enrich the dough with ingredients such as beaten eggs and yoghurt and these should be added at this stage.

4 Add the dry ingredients: Sprinkle over the flour in an even layer, ensuring that all the liquid is covered. If you are adding skimmed milk powder, more than 2 tbsp of sugar or spices, add about half of the flour, then the extra dry ingredients, then the rest of the flour. Add the salt and sugar to the pan, placing them in opposite corners, then make a small hollow in the middle of the flour.

5 Add the yeast: Put the yeast in the hollow you have made in the flour. It is important that it does not come into contact with the salt, sugar or liquid at this point. This is particularly important if you are planning to use the delay timer as the yeast would be activated before the dough is mixed.

6 Put the bread pan in the breadmaker: Put the bread pan into the bread machine, fitting it firmly in place and folding the handle down. If your machine has an automatic dispenser, you can put ingredients such as seeds, fruit and nuts in it and slot it into place in the lid of the machine. Close the lid. Plug in the socket and switch on the power.

7 Select a programme: Select your desired programme from the control panel. If available, you can also choose a crust setting at this stage – light, medium or dark – and the size of the loaf – small (425–450g), medium (700–850g) or large (875g–1kg). Your machine will cook a small loaf for less time than a large one, and a light crust for less time than a dark one, so it is important you make these selections if available.

8 Add additional ingredients: If your machine doesn't have an automatic dispenser, add ingredients such as dried fruit, seeds and nuts when the bleeper sounds during the second kneading or, if your machine doesn't have a bleeper, about halfway through the kneading time.

9 Glaze the loaf and add toppings: If you want to brush the loaf with beaten egg, milk or water, or add toppings such as oats, or seeds, do this when the bread has finished its last proving and just before baking. Try to keep the lid open for as little time as possible to retain the heat, then close the lid carefully.

10 After baking: At the end of the cycle, your machine may bleep to alert you that it is ready. Remember that both the bread and the inside of the machine will be very hot. Open the lid carefully and lift out the bread pan, holding it by the handle with oven-gloved hands. Put the bread pan on a heatproof surface (the base will also be extremely hot) for 2–3 minutes to let it settle.

11 Turn out the bread: Still using oven gloves, turn the pan upside-down and gently shake it to release the bread. Place the bread on its base on a wire rack so you don't crush or crack the top of the loaf.

12 Leave to cool: If the kneading paddle has not remained in the bread pan and is embedded inside the bread, leave to cool for about 20 minutes, then carefully prise the blade from the loaf using a utensil that won't scratch or damage the non-stick blade, such as a wooden or rigid plastic spatula. Serve the bread warm or leave to cool completely before storing.

Top *baker's tips* for success – getting the most from your machine

- Before you make your first loaf, read your bread machine manual thoroughly; it should explain how your particular machine works, exactly what all the symbols on the control panel mean, and any extras that are unique to the model you have chosen.
- Use good-quality fresh ingredients and check that everything is within its use-by date. Some flours, particularly organic ones, seeds and nuts have a relatively short shelf-life and can go stale or even rancid; yeast past its expiry date will produce poorer results.
- Tap water can have an adverse effect on yeast (and bread flavour) if it contains a lot of chlorine. If you can smell and taste chlorine in a glass of tap water, use spring water, filtered water or cooled boiled water instead.
- Measure accurately; it doesn't take very long. Use weighing scales for dry ingredients, a detailed measuring jug and proper measuring spoons rather than just a teaspoon and tablespoon from your cutlery drawer. This is particularly important with yeast.
- Add the ingredients in the sequence given in the recipe (unless your machine's manual states otherwise) and don't exceed the quantities of flour and liquid recommended for your machine; if you have too much dough, it may rise over the top of the bread pan.
- When using the delay timer, avoid perishable ingredients such as fresh milk, eggs, cheese and meat. Instead of milk, you can use a combination of water and milk powder.
- Check the dough after the first 5 minutes of mixing, especially when you are trying out a new recipe. Bread machine dough should be slightly wetter than if you mix it by hand, but the dryness of flour can vary. At this stage you can add a little more flour if the dough is wet and sticky or a little more water if it looks crumbly. Keep a flexible rubber spatula to hand and, if necessary, scrape down the sides as the kneading blade sometimes fails to pick up dough from the corners of the pan.
- Although it's tempting to check the progress of your loaf, don't lift the lid during the proving and baking stages as this will let out heat and steam and your bread may not rise as well. Many machines come with a viewing window (although this can get very steamed up) and a light, so you can see how well your loaf is doing.
- Keep your bread machine clean. After use, the bread pan and kneading blade should be carefully washed in hot soapy water, using a scourer suitable for non-stick cookware, if necessary. Always remove the kneading blade for washing as tiny pieces of dough can get trapped underneath. If you find it difficult to remove the kneading blade from the pan after taking out the bread, half fill the pan with warm water and leave to soak for about 10 minutes before easing the blade off. Never immerse the base of the bread pan in water or put it in a dishwasher.
- Be prepared to experiment, which will of course mean some less successful loaves; but it's the only way to discover new flavours and breads.

Choosing Ingredients for Bread Machine Baking

Before you use your bread machine, it is useful to understand the basic principles of bread-making, know what ingredients are suitable and the results you can expect from them. Most of the ingredients mentioned here are available in supermarkets and health food shops; or can be bought by mail order.

Flour

For well-risen bread, it is essential to use flour that has been milled from 'hard' wheat, usually labelled 'strong' or 'bread' flour. Hard grains are used in strong bread flours because they contain the most protein, which determines how much gluten can be developed during kneading. Gluten absorbs water and forms an elastic, stringy network within the dough, which sets in the heat of the oven during baking, giving bread its light and airy texture. Alternatively, you can mix flours with a low gluten content with a flour that contains more gluten.

Strong white bread flour: This is used in the majority of recipes in this book. It is ground from the wheat kernel once the outer bran is removed. Check the protein content on the side of the flour packet and look for one in the range 10.5–14 per cent.

Very strong white bread flour: With a slightly higher protein content (up to 15 per cent), this is particularly good when blending white bread flour with lower-gluten flours to achieve the maximum rise.

Unbleached strong white bread flour: Most white flour is bleached to whiten and to age it quickly, ready for use in cooking. This flour is untreated and has a slightly creamy colour; it is left to age naturally to develop the baking qualities.

Strong wholemeal bread flour: Sometimes known as strong wholewheat bread flour, this is made by grinding the wholewheat kernel. It has a coarser texture than white flour, more flavour and more nutrients. Because the bran inhibits the gluten development, the dough will rise more slowly, so the programme cycle will be longer. For bread machine baking, it's best to use a proportion of strong white bread flour along with wholemeal bread flour to achieve a lighter texture. Wholemeal flours vary in coarseness and may be stoneground (the finest milled), or medium or coarsely milled; the latter making roughly textured loaves.

Strong brown bread flour: This has some of the bran removed and usually contains around 85 per cent of the wholewheat kernel. The texture is much finer than wholemeal flour.

Kamut and Einkorn flours: These are ancient varieties of wheat, usually ground into wholegrain organic flour. Einkorn was the original wheat which grew over 20,000 years ago and was once a staple across the Mediterranean. Kamut was first grown by the pharaohs in Egypt and is naturally high in protein (around 15 per cent) and minerals such as selenium. These organic wholegrain flours have a distinctive flavour and produce beautifully golden loaves. They can be used in place of ordinary wholemeal flour in any of the recipes in this book.

Spelt flour: Either white or wholegrain, spelt flour is also derived from an ancient form of wheat and ground into an organic flour that makes superb bread with a rich, nutty flavour. Slightly higher in protein, vitamins and minerals than ordinary wheat flour, it can sometimes be tolerated by people with wheat allergies.

French white flour: Made from varieties of wheat particular to France. Type 55 is ideal for making baguettes as it makes loaves with a light, open texture and crisp crust. Use on the bread machine French bread setting for breads with no added fat or sugar.

Rye flour: Once a staple in northern, eastern and central Europe where soils were too poor to grow wheat, this features widely in breads from Scandinavia, Germany and Russia. This grey-brown flour makes dark, close-textured bread with a distinctive flavour. Low in gluten, rye flour must be mixed with strong white flour in the bread machine. If you use a high proportion of rye flour, you also need an acidic element such as buttermilk, yoghurt or a sourdough starter to break down the starch so that water can be absorbed by the dough. Dark rye flour is made from the wholegrain; light rye is made by sifting out some of the bran.

Barley and Barleycorn flour: With a mild and slightly sweet flavour, barley flour makes loaves with a soft texture. It is low in gluten, so must be mixed with strong white flour for bread machine baking. Barleycorn flour is a combination of wheat and barley flour with malted barley flakes and linseeds.

Granary and Malthouse flours: A blend of wholemeal and white flour mixed with malted wheat grains gives a nutty and slightly sweet flavour.

Buckwheat flour: This isn't a wheat flour at all but is milled from a seed related to the rhubarb family. A greyish-brown flour, it has a pronounced earthy flavour and is low in gluten, so should be mixed with strong bread flours to help it rise.

Gluten-free flours: Available in white and brown blends and containing a mixture of starches, gluten-free flours are made from potato, rice and soya flour, plus added natural gum, usually xanthan gum. Bread made with this flour is very different from ordinary wheat bread and often has a denser texture and less risen finish, but is a good alternative if you cannot tolerate gluten. Only gluten-free flours that are specifically designed for bread-making are suitable for the bread machine.

Other grains and products

Oatmeal: Finer than rolled oats, this is made from oat kernels or 'groats' cut into pieces to make fine, medium or coarse oatmeal or fully ground to make flour. Oatmeal contains no gluten, so must be mixed with wheat flour for making bread. You can also add oat bran to bread for extra texture and fibre, but only use a maximum of 2 tbsp per 250g flour as it inhibits the development of gluten.

Rolled oats: Oats add a chewy texture and nutty taste to bread and make an attractive topping. You can get jumbo-size oat flakes as well as traditional rolled oats and these are a better choice than quick-cook oats.

Unsweetened muesli: This is a great way to add rolled oats, wheat flakes, chopped nuts and dried fruits to bread without buying the individual items.

Wheatgerm: This is the germ (the part from which the plant grows) of the wheat grain which is removed when making white flour and sold separately. It is highly nutritious and a good source of vitamins B and E and fibre, but does not keep for long. Store in an airtight container in a cool dry place or in the freezer if you have space.

Flavourings

All manner of flavourings and seasonings can transform a plain loaf into something special. Many recipes suggest adding flavourings part-way through kneading (or via an automatic dispenser) to prevent the ingredients being crushed into smaller pieces during mixing and extra wear on the non-stick bread pan, but if it is more convenient, it is fine to add them with the flour at the beginning of the programme.

Salt: Salt not only enhances the flavour of the bread but is important for controlling the rate at which the yeast works. This strengthens the gluten and stops the bread rising too rapidly, then collapsing; for this reason it is better not to use salt substitutes. Using too much salt will inhibit the yeast, so be careful when adding additional salty ingredients such as olives or cheese.

Cold meats: Well-flavoured chopped deli meats – such as chorizo, bacon or salami – can all be used in bread.

Herbs: Add fresh chopped herbs to your dough, or seasonings such as chilli flakes or ground or crushed spices. If you are using dried herbs, substitute 1 tsp dried for every 1 tbsp fresh.

Seeds: Lightly toast seeds – such as pumpkin, sunflower and sesame – and chopped nuts by dry-frying in a non-stick pan for a few minutes (taking care not to allow them to burn) to bring out their flavour.

Vegetables: You can also add grated or finely chopped raw and cooked vegetable or fruit purées as well as soaked, dried vegetables. If you do, make sure you adjust the liquid in the recipe or the dough will be too wet. Use fresh garlic very sparingly in bread recipes as its anti-fungal properties inhibit the action of the yeast. For a stronger garlic flavour, use dried garlic powder or garlic-flavoured salt.

Raising agents

Yeast: Only fast-action (easy-blend) yeast is suitable for using in bread machines and doesn't need to be activated before use. These tiny granules of 'instant' yeast are readily available in supermarkets and come in small vacuum packets or boxes of individual sachets, each containing about 7g or 2½tsp. The sachets contain added ascorbic acid (vitamin C), which increases the strength of the gluten, so that the dough rises more. Always check the 'sell by' date when using yeast, as it doesn't keep long. Fast-action dried yeast should be added to the dry ingredients and kept away from the liquid, salt and sugar until mixing begins.

Sourdough starter: Bread made using the sourdough method has a distinctive, slightly acidic flavour and a more aerated texture. The recipe below contains dried yeast, although traditionally it would have been made without commercial yeast, and the flour and water mixture would have relied on natural yeasts present in the air and on the flour. When you have used some of your starter, you will need to 'feed' and replenish it; providing you do this, it should keep indefinitely.

Sourdough starter

250g strong white bread flour
2 tsp fast-action dried yeast
300ml water

- Put the flour and yeast in a large bowl and stir together. Make a hollow in the middle and add the water. Gradually blend in with a wooden spoon or whisk to make a thick batter.
- Cover with a clean tea towel or piece of muslin and leave undisturbed in a cool room, away from direct sunlight for 3–5 days to ferment. The batter is ready when it is frothy and has a pleasantly sour smell. Cover the bowl with clingfilm and store in the fridge.
- Before using the starter, remove from the fridge and leave for about 30 minutes to reach room temperature. Stir the batter, then remove the amount required with a ladle.
- Replenish the starter by the amount you have removed (you need to do this at least every two weeks). For example, if you have used 300ml, you will need to add 150ml water and 150g flour. Let this ferment at room temperature as before for 24 hours, then store in the fridge.

Liquids

Unless your machine's manual states otherwise, liquids can be cold when they are added to the bread pan as many machines have a preheat function before mixing. Sometimes, when the bread is being prepared on a rapid or quick setting, you need to add warm liquid as the cycle is so short. Any liquid should just feel warm to your little finger; if it is too hot the yeast will be killed.

Water: The most commonly used liquid when making bread, tap water is fine, but if water has been heavily chlorinated or fluorinated, this may slow down rising and you may wish to use filtered, boiled and cooled water or bottled spring water instead.

Milk: Milk enriches the dough and gives a softer result. Use full-cream, semi-skimmed or skimmed milk, according to your preference. (Lacto-free milk, soya milk and rice milks are also fine for those on lactose-free or dairy-free diets.) Fresh milk can be replaced with skimmed milk powder and water; useful if you intend to use the timer to delay the starting time for making bread. Sprinkle the powder between two layers of flour so that it does not come in contact with the water.

Buttermilk and plain yoghurt: Both of these can also be used, either on their own or in combination with fresh milk or water. These give bread a tangy flavour and a moister, more cake-like texture.

Coconut milk: Especially good in sweet breads, this is best diluted with water. As it is high in fat, adjust the amount of butter or oil you use in the bread.

Fruit and vegetable juices: Adding both flavour and colour, you can add leftover cooking liquid from vegetables; potato water is especially good as it contains starch. If you salt your water when cooking vegetables, you may need to adjust the amount of salt you add to the bread mixture.

Beer and ale: With a good affinity with dark heavier breads such as rye bread, this adds a distinctive flavour and extra colour.

Eggs: Often used in rich, buttery loaves such as brioche and sweet breads, eggs add colour and extra nutritional value. Beat in a measuring jug so that you can top up with liquid to the quantity required in the recipe.

Fats

A small amount of fat is added to most breads to improve the flavour, texture and keeping qualities. It can be solid, such as butter or margarine, or liquid such as sunflower or olive oil. The recipes in this book were tested with salted butter, but you can use unsalted butter (you may wish to add a little extra salt to the recipe), margarine or dairy-free spread if you prefer. Avoid reduced-fat spreads as they have a higher water content and the dough will become too soft; if you want to cut down the fat in a recipe, add 1 tbsp extra water for every 15g of fat you remove. You can also substitute sunflower or rapeseed oil in recipes which call for 40g of butter or less (substitute 1 tbsp oil for each 15g butter). Nut oils such as walnut and hazelnut are expensive, but add a subtle flavouring to breads which do not have other strong flavours (which would simply mask their flavour).

Sweeteners

Most recipes, whether sweet or savoury, contain a small amount of sugar or other sweetener. This enhances the flavour and helps activate the yeast to start the dough rising. It also delays the staling process in bread because it attracts moisture. Adding sugar darkens the crust of the finished loaf, so where recipes include more than 3 tbsp sugar, you should either use a sweet bread programme (which has a lower baking temperature), or the basic programme with a light crust setting.

Sugar: Most types of sugar can be used for bread-making. White granulated or caster sugar add sweetness but no flavour, or you can add light or dark brown sugar, either refined or muscovado, for a touch of colour and flavour.

Honey and liquid sweeteners: Honey, maple syrup and golden syrup can all be used instead of sugar. Black treacle, molasses and malt extract all add sweetness, but also a dark colour and stronger taste; they are often used in conjunction with wholemeal and rye flours.

Special bread additives

There are a number of commercially made conditioners which can be added to bread dough to improve the rise or texture of the loaf.

Dough enhancer (or dough improver): A powdered organic mixture which contains wheat flour, flour treatment agent and ascorbic acid (vitamin C), this improves the strength of the gluten and conditions the dough to create a better texture. Add 1–2 tsp to 500g wholemeal, rye or other whole grain flours, or use in white bread flour recipes with heavy ingredients such as cheese.

Dough softener (or dough relaxer): A mixture of wheat flour and vegetable oil, this softens the gluten to make softer and moister breads and rolls with better keeping qualities. Add 1–2 tsp to 500g white, wholemeal or other flour.

Vital wheat gluten: This adds extra gluten to low-gluten flours. Add 1–2 tbsp per 500g of flour. It's not recommended for use with white flours unless the mixture contains heavy ingredients such as cheese, nuts or seeds.

Ascorbic acid (vitamin C) powder: This may help wholemeal breads to rise to a lighter texture. It is often already added to bread flours and fast-action yeast, so check this before adding more. Add 1 tsp to 500g of flour. Lemon juice may act in the same way; add 1 tsp with the liquid.

Using bread mixes

A huge range of ready-prepared bread mixes is available and can be useful if you want to try flavoured bread such as mixed seed, or chilli and dried peppers, but prefer not to buy the individual ingredients. Some mixes include yeast and simply need the addition of water; others are flour mixes and need the addition of both yeast and liquid. Read the packet instructions carefully as not all bread mixes are suitable for bread machines. Refer to your bread machine manual as well as the packet before using ready-prepared bread mixes, as some bread machines have a specific programme for this. Above all, make sure that your machine can cope with the volume of ingredients being used.

Conversion charts

This book provides metric measurements for the ingredients, but those who still prefer Imperial, or who want to use US measures, can use these conversions.
If you use American cup measures, an American cup is 250ml of liquid, or whatever volume fits into the space, so the same weight of two different ingredients will have different cup measures, for example, 1 cup of flour is 100g while 1 cup of butter is 225g.

WEIGHT	
Metric	Imperial
25g	1oz
50g	2oz
75g	3oz
100g	4oz
150g	5oz
175g	6oz
200g	7oz
225g	8oz
250g	9oz
300g	10oz
350g	12oz
400g	14oz
450g	1lb

LIQUID MEASURE		
Metric	Imperial	US cup
5ml	1 tsp	1 tsp
15ml	1 tbsp	1 tbsp
50ml	2fl oz	3 tbsp
60ml	2½fl oz	¼ tbsp
75ml	3fl oz	⅓ cup
100ml	4fl oz	scant ½ cup
125ml	4½fl oz	½ cup
150ml	5fl oz	⅔ cup
200ml	7fl oz	scant 1 cup
250ml	10fl oz	1 cup
300ml	½pt	1¼ cups
350ml	12fl oz	1⅓ cups
450ml	¾pt	1¾ cups
500ml	20fl oz	2 cups
600ml	1pt	2½ cups

OVEN TEMPERATURES		
°C		°F
110°C	Gas ¼	225°F
120°C	Gas ½	250°F
140°C	Gas 1	275°F
150°C	Gas 2	300°F
160°C	Gas 3	325°F
180°C	Gas 4	350°F
190°C	Gas 5	375°F
200°C	Gas 6	400°F
220°C	Gas 7	425°F
230°C	Gas 8	450°F
240°C	Gas 9	475°F

MEASUREMENTS	
Metric	Imperial
5cm	2in
10cm	4in
13cm	5in
15cm	6in
18cm	7in
20cm	8in
25cm	10in
30cm	12in

CHAPTER 3

Finishing and Storing

Once you have made your loaves, give a little thought to presentation, and make sure you store your bread properly so you don't waste any of it.

How to glaze and finish bread

Most of the breads in this book are left plain and unglazed; after all, bread machines are all about fuss-free bread baking. However, when you have the time, a simple brushed-on glaze or quickly scattered topping can add the final flourish to your loaf.

Flour: A sprinkling of flour gives a loaf a farmhouse-style finish and keeps the crust soft. Sprinkle with a little sifted white flour just before baking or use wholemeal, brown or Granary flour for a rustic look. Brush the loaf with water or milk first if you want the flour to stay in place after baking. If you forget to flour the top before baking, you can sprinkle a little over the cooked loaf while it is still hot.

Water: You can use water to create a crisper crust; just brush or spray it over the loaf with a mister just before baking. It's traditionally used for French-style bread with little added fat or sugar. You can also make a salty or sweet glaze by stirring ½ tsp salt or caster sugar into 2 tbsp warm water.

Milk: Brushing with milk gives a soft, slightly shiny glaze and is popular on white loaves and sweet breads. Brush over just before baking.

Egg glaze: Use this to add a golden colour and glossy appearance. For savoury loaves, beat 1 egg, 2 tsp water and a pinch of salt together; for an even richer colour, just use the egg yolk. For sweet loaves, use sugar instead of salt. An egg white can also be used as a glaze if you brush a little beaten white over the loaf as soon as it is turned out; the egg will cook in the residual heat to a clear, shiny finish.

Oil and melted butter: Either of these can be brushed over bread while still hot to soften the crust. Use a good quality-olive oil on breads such as focaccia, or try hazelnut or walnut oils on nut or seed breads. Melted butter is particularly good on bread rolls.

Honey and maple syrup: Either of these can be brushed over sweet baked bread and buns for a sweet sticky glaze. There's no need to heat them first as they will become runnier with the warmth of the bread.

Other toppings

Breads can be sprinkled with a whole range of toppings just before baking. Glaze first with water, milk or egg, then for savoury loaves scatter with seeds, chopped or flaked nuts, cornmeal (polenta), wheat or oat flakes or grated cheese. You could also add a light dusting of paprika or sea salt. For sweet loaves, nuts and sugar (such as Demerara) look attractive, or after baking you could glaze with honey or syrup and scatter with chopped candied fruits or toasted nuts. A dusting of icing sugar also looks good, but unless you are planning to serve the loaf warm, do this when the bread is completely cool or moisture will make it disolve and go sticky.

How to adapt your own bread recipes

If you want to adapt a favourite bread recipe, not originally meant for a bread machine, base the ingredients and method on one of the recipes in this book that you have made and know works well in your machine, or find a similar recipe in your bread machine manual, so that you know which bread programme to use. Recipes are usually simple to adapt for bread machines, following these few simple rules.

- Make sure the quantity will work in your bread machine; if you have a compact machine it may be necessary to reduce the size of the loaf. Each model will have a maximum capacity, so check in your bread machine manual. When reducing quantities, it's vital to keep the flour and liquid in the right proportions. You can be a bit more flexible with flavouring ingredients such as nuts and spices.
- If your recipe contains fresh yeast, replace it with fast-action dried yeast; 6g fresh yeast equals 1 tsp dried yeast. In white flour breads, use 1–1¼ tsp fast-action dried yeast per 450–500g flour; in white flour breads with a lot of ingredients such as butter, cheese or

fruit and in brown and wholemeal breads, you will need about 1½ tsp per 450–500g flour.

- Additions such as dried fruit and nuts mean that the dough will take longer to rise. Limit these to no more than a quarter of the weight of the flour.
- High sugar levels may make your bread over-brown. Use a maximum of 50g sugar, or ingredients such as golden syrup or malt extract, per 450–500g flour. If you are reducing the amount of liquid sweeteners and syrups, you may need to add a spoonful or two of extra liquid to compensate. For sweet breads, use the light crust setting.
- When adding ingredients to the bread pan, pour in the liquid first (unless your bread machine's manual says otherwise), then add the fat and beaten egg, if included in your recipe, followed by about half the flour. Add other ingredients such as sugar or other sweetener (if more than 1 tbsp), dried fruit, nuts, grated cheese, etc., then the rest of the flour. Put the salt and sugar (if less than 1 tbsp) in separate corners of the bread pan, then make a hollow in the middle of the flour and add the yeast.
- Check the dough when the machine starts mixing as bread machine dough is usually a little softer than those made by hand, as the dough blade needs to able to mix easily without straining the motor. You may need to add a little more liquid or flour to get the consistency right; do this a tablespoon at a time.

How to cool, store and freeze baked bread

Removing your loaf from the bread pan: As soon as baking is complete, the loaf is best removed from the machine as soon as possible, as condensation that occurs as the machine cools may make the bread soggy. Cover the top of the hot bread with a clean tea towel, leave for about 30 seconds, as a tiny amount of steam will loosen the sides, then turn the pan upside-down, holding it with oven gloves and shaking gently to release the bread onto a cooling rack. Turn the bread on its base and leave it to cool completely, or for at least 30 minutes, before slicing.

If the bread is stuck in the pan, gently loosen the sides with a plastic spatula; don't try to free the loaf with a knife or you will scratch the non-stick coating. If the kneading blade gets stuck inside the loaf after baking, carefully ease it out after 15–30 minutes, or as soon as the bread is cool enough to handle. If you find it difficult to remove the kneading blade from the bread pan after taking out the bread, half fill the pan with warm water and leave to soak for about 15 minutes before easing the blade away.

Storing bread: A freshly baked loaf is best eaten within two days, as unlike commercially made bread, it contains no added preservatives. Once the bread has cooled, wrap it in a food-safe plastic bag, and seal it well. Keep in a cool place, but not in the fridge as this dries out the loaf and makes it stale more quickly. Breads with a crisp crust will soften if wrapped, so until you cut into the loaf, they are best left unwrapped, covered with a clean tea towel. There are lots of products available to keep bread fresh including breathable bread bags with perforations that allow moisture to escape, to keep the crust crisp and to slow down staling, and bread boxes with airtight lids.

Freezing bread: For longer storage, freezing is the best option, ideally as soon as the loaf has cooled. Leave whole and place in a large freezer bag, or slice for convenience so that you can remove a few slices at a time, when you need them. Seal the bag and freeze for up to 3 months. Thaw the bread at room temperature, still in the freezer bag.

Troubleshooting

Bread machines are simple to use, but occasionally you will turn out a loaf that may not be quite as perfect as you'd like. To make sure it doesn't happen again, here are a few troubleshooting baker's tips.

The bread did not rise well. Why?

- Not enough yeast was added, the yeast wasn't fresh, or it came in contact with the salt, sugar or liquid before the mixing started. Check the sell-by date on the yeast and once a packet of yeast is opened, use as soon as possible as it stales quickly.
- If you were using warm water, the water was too hot and so killed the yeast. The water should be 21–28°C – just warm or tepid to the touch. If in doubt, dip your little finger in the water; you should be able to keep it there comfortably for 5 seconds.
- The ingredients were very cold at the start of mixing. On very cold days, let tap water stand at room temperature for about 20 minutes before using (or microwave for a few seconds) and do the same with fridge ingredients such as milk and butter.
- You used too little sugar or too much salt. A little sugar helps activate the yeast, which is why it is included in most recipes, but don't use too much or it will have the opposite effect! Too much salt can slow the growth of the yeast.
- Too much of another ingredient, such as bran or garlic, has inhibited the yeast. Use less next time and add a couple of teaspoons of dough improver to help heavier breads to rise.

Why has the top of the loaf stuck to the lid of the machine?

- Too much mixture for the size of your bread machine. Scale down the ingredients next time.
- Too much yeast. Always use accurate measuring spoons.

- Insufficient salt; salt helps to prevent the dough from rising too quickly or over-proving.
- High humidity and/or very warm weather. The bread machine isn't a sealed, airtight unit, and will be affected by the temperature in the room. When very hot, use just a tiny bit less yeast.

Why doesn't the bread have a rounded top?
- Too much liquid or yeast or too little salt. All these may have made the bread rise quickly and then collapse.
- The bread machine was jolted, or the lid was opened during proving or baking, making the loaf sink a little. If you need to open the lid to glaze or add a topping, make sure you do so just as the baking starts and keep it open for as little time as possible.
- Not all loaves are meant have a domed surface after baking. Those that contain a high proportion of wholemeal, brown or rye flour or highly enriched breads are more likely to have a flat or craggy surface or even a slightly sunken one. This won't affect the flavour of the finished bread.

Why is the texture heavy?
- It could be that there was not enough yeast or not enough liquid so that the dough was unable to stretch as the yeast expanded.
- Additional ingredients, such as grated vegetables or fruit purée contained a lot of moisture. Always reduce the amount of additional liquid when adding moist ingredients.

Why is the texture of the loaf crumbly and dry?
- Too little liquid was added or ingredients such as grains or bran have soaked up more liquid than expected. Increase the liquid quantity slightly or reduce quantity of additional ingredients. Check the dough during mixing and if it looks dry, add more liquid, a tablespoon at a time.

Why is the crust burnt?
- There was too much sugar or other sweetener, such as honey or syrup, in the dough. Use less or use the sweet bread programme if your machine offers this option, which cooks at a slightly lower temperature.
- You selected a dark crust setting on a loaf which contained more than 1 tbsp sugar or 100ml milk. Both of these darken the crust, so use a light or medium crust setting.

Why is the top of the bread pale?

- You may have selected the light crust setting. Use medium or dark next time.
- There may be little sugar in the mixture. Increase a little and add a spoonful of dried skimmed milk with the dry ingredients. Or, brush the top with egg glaze just before baking.
- Wheat and gluten-free breads tend to have very pale tops. You can brush the tops with a little butter and brown for a minute or two under a hot grill, if you like.

How can I get a crisper crust?

- Use water rather than milk and less fat in the mixture.
- Select the French bread programme.
- Turn the bread out of the bread pan onto a wire rack as soon as baking is completed.

How can I get a softer crust?

- Use milk instead of water and add a little more fat to the mixture.
- Use a dough softener (see page 26).
- Turn the bread out onto a wire rack and loosely cover with a clean tea towel while it cools.

Everyday Basic Bread

Here you'll find a selection of the simplest breads from a straightforward white loaf to basic brown bread and traditional wholemeal. These are for everyday use, perfect toasted for breakfast and ideal for sandwiches and quick snacks. To reflect the popularity of breads with added seeds, there's a speedy seeded loaf cooked on the rapid programme for those who need a freshly baked loaf in as little time as possible. For those on a tight budget, this chapter includes an economy white loaf which makes use of supermarket 'value' flour. These are some of the easiest breads to make, and if you haven't baked a loaf in your bread machine before, then this is the place to start.

Simple White Loaf

Ingredients:
325ml water
2 tbsp sunflower oil
500g plus 1 tsp strong white
   bread flour
1¼ tsp salt
1 tbsp caster sugar
1 tsp fast-action dried yeast

Quantities for a large (900g)
*   loaf*
390ml water
2 tbsp sunflower oil
600g plus 1 tsp strong white
   bread flour
1½ tsp salt
4 tsp caster sugar
1½ tsp fast-action dried
   yeast.

Quantities for a small (450g)
*   loaf*
195ml water
1 tbsp sunflower oil
300g plus ½ tsp strong
   white bread flour
¾ tsp salt
2 tsp caster sugar
¾ tsp fast-action dried yeast

This straightforward recipe produces a perfect, well-risen loaf. Inside, it is soft and light with an open texture, while the golden crust is finished with a very light dusting of flour. This makes an excellent starting point if you are new to bread machine baking.

- Lift the bread pan out of the bread machine and fit the kneading blade. Pour in the water, then add the oil, followed by the 500g flour.
- Put the salt and sugar in separate corners of the pan, then make a shallow dip in the middle of the flour and add the yeast.
- Fit the pan into the bread machine, shut the lid and set to the basic white setting with a crust of your choice. Press start.
- After baking, lift the pan out of the machine using oven gloves. Carefully shake out the loaf to remove it from the pan, then transfer to a wire rack, standing the loaf on its base.
- Lightly dust the top with the remaining 1 tsp flour while the loaf is hot. Leave to cool.

Baker's tip
- If preferred, you can brush the top of the dough with water and sprinkle with the flour just before baking starts. Alternatively, leave the crust plain and unfloured.

Makes a 800g loaf

Traditional Wholemeal Bread

This wholemeal loaf has a fairly heavy and close texture. Made from the complete wheat kernel, wholemeal flour makes a more nutritious and fuller-flavoured bread than white, but the extra bran hinders rising, so a little more yeast is needed for good results.

- Lift the bread pan out of the bread machine and fit the kneading blade. Pour in the water, then add the oil, followed by the flour.
- Put the salt and sugar in separate corners of the pan, then make a shallow dip in the middle of the flour and add the yeast.
- Fit the pan into the bread machine, shut the lid and set to the wholewheat setting with a crust of your choice. Press start.
- After baking, lift the pan out of the machine using oven gloves. Carefully shake out the loaf to remove it from the pan, then transfer to a wire rack, standing the loaf on its base. Leave to cool.

Baker's tip
- Vitamin C (ascorbic acid) is often added to wholemeal bread mixes to improve the volume of the loaf. Fast-action dried yeast usually contains this, but you may add a little extra to improve results. Try adding ¼ tsp vitamin C powder or ½ finely crushed vitamin C tablet to the flour. Alternatively, use 1–2 tsp commercial dough improver (See page 25).

Ingredients:
350ml water
2 tbsp sunflower oil
500g strong wholemeal
   bread flour
1½ tsp salt
1 tbsp light soft brown
   sugar
1½ tsp fast-action dried
   yeast

*Quantities for a large
   (950g) loaf*
420ml water
2 tbsp sunflower oil
600g strong wholemeal
   bread flour
1½ tsp salt
4 tsp light soft brown sugar
1¾ tsp fast-action dried
   yeast

*Quantities for a small
   (475g) loaf*
210ml water
1 tbsp sunflower oil
300g strong wholemeal
   bread flour
¾ tsp salt
2 tsp light soft brown sugar
¾ tsp fast-action dried
   yeast

Light Wholemeal Loaf

Machine-baked bread made entirely from wholemeal flour tends to have a fairly heavy texture. Adding a proportion of white flour makes the dough much lighter, while the bread still keeps a traditional wholemeal flavour and appearance.

Ingredients:
350ml water
25g butter, at room
    temperature
350g strong wholemeal
    bread flour
150g strong white bread
    flour
1½ tsp salt
1 tbsp light soft brown sugar
1½ tsp fast-action dried
    yeast

Quantities for a large
    (950g) loaf
420ml water
30g butter
425g strong wholemeal
    bread flour
175g strong white bread
    flour
1½ tsp salt
4 tsp light soft brown sugar
1¾ tsp fast-action dried
    yeast

Quantities for a small
    (475g) loaf
210ml water
15g butter
200g strong wholemeal
    bread flour
100g strong white bread
    flour
½ tsp salt
2 tsp light soft brown sugar
¾ tsp fast-action dried yeast

- Lift the bread pan out of the bread machine and fit the kneading blade. Pour in the water, then add the butter, followed by the flours.
- Put the salt and sugar in separate corners of the pan, then make a shallow dip in the middle of the flour and add the yeast.
- Fit the pan into the bread machine, shut the lid and set to the wholewheat setting with a crust of your choice. Press start.
- After baking, lift the pan out of the machine using oven gloves. Carefully shake out the loaf to remove it from the pan, then transfer to a wire rack, standing the loaf on its base. Leave to cool.

Baker's tip
- For a slightly darker colour and richer flavour, use dark soft brown or muscovado sugar.

Light Seeded Wholemeal Loaf

Adding an assortment of seeds to bread is a great way to add taste and texture plus nutritional value. This mixture also contains milk powder, which gives the bread a slightly softer texture and darker crust, so use a light or medium crust setting.

- Lift the bread pan out of the bread machine and fit the kneading blade. Pour in the water, then add the oil, followed by the strong wholemeal bread flour. Reserve 1 tbsp mixed seeds, then sprinkle the rest over the flour. Sprinkle over the milk powder, followed by the strong white bread flour.
- Put the salt and sugar in separate corners of the pan, then make a shallow dip in the middle of the flour and add the yeast.
- Fit the pan into the bread machine, shut the lid and set to the wholewheat setting with a light or medium crust. Press start.
- Just before baking begins, brush the top of the loaf with milk and sprinkle with the reserved seeds.
- After baking, lift the pan out of the machine using oven gloves. Carefully shake out the loaf to remove it from the pan, then transfer to a wire rack, standing the loaf on its base. Leave to cool.

Ingredients:
300ml water
2 tbsp sunflower oil
300g strong wholemeal bread flour
2 tbsp sunflower seeds
2 tbsp pumpkin seeds
1 tbsp poppy seeds
1 tbsp sesame seeds
2 tbsp skimmed milk powder
175g strong white bread flour
1¼ tsp salt
2 tsp soft light brown sugar
1¼ tsp fast-action dried yeast
1 tbsp milk, to glaze

Quantities for a large (900g) loaf
360ml water
2 tbsp sunflower oil
350g strong wholemeal bread flour
30g sunflower seeds
30g pumpkin seeds
4 tsp poppy seeds
4 tsp sesame seeds
2½ tbsp skimmed milk powder
220g strong white bread flour
1½ tsp salt
1 tbsp soft light brown sugar
1½ tsp fast-action dried yeast
4 tsp milk, to glaze

Quantities for a small (450g) loaf
180ml water
1 tbsp sunflower oil
175g strong wholemeal bread flour
15g sunflower seeds
15g pumpkin seeds
2 tsp poppy seeds
2 tsp sesame seeds
1 tbsp skimmed milk powder
110g strong white bread flour
¾ tsp salt
1½ tsp soft light brown sugar
¾ tsp fast-action dried yeast
2 tsp milk, to glaze

Half and Half Loaf

Ingredients:
350ml lukewarm water
2 tbsp sunflower oil
250g strong wholemeal
    bread flour
250g strong white bread
    flour
1½ tsp salt
1 tbsp caster sugar
1½ tsp fast-action dried
    yeast

*Quantities for a large
    (900g) loaf*
420ml water
2 tbsp sunflower oil
300g strong wholemeal
    bread flour
300g strong white bread
    flour
1½ tsp salt
4 tsp caster sugar
1½ tsp fast-action dried
    yeast.

*Quantities for a small
    (450g) loaf*
210ml water
1 tbsp sunflower oil
150g strong wholemeal
    bread flour
150g strong white bread
    flour
¾ tsp salt
2 tsp caster sugar
¾ tsp fast-action dried yeast

This is a great compromise for those who feel that wholemeal bread is healthier, but prefer the taste and texture of white! Serve toasted at breakfast time for a great start to the day, or use for lunchtime sandwiches; the loaf is less crumbly than a wholemeal loaf.

- Lift the bread pan out of the bread machine and fit the kneading blade. Pour in the water, then add the oil, followed by the wholemeal and white bread flour.
- Put the salt and sugar in separate corners of the pan, then make a shallow dip in the middle of the flour and add the yeast.
- Fit the pan into the bread machine, shut the lid and set to the basic white setting with a crust of your choice. Press start.
- After baking, lift the pan out of the machine using oven gloves. Carefully shake out the loaf to remove it from the pan, then transfer to a wire rack, standing the loaf on its base. Leave to cool.

Baker's tip
- When using a proportion of wholemeal flour and the basic white setting, adding slightly warm rather than cold water will allow the dough to start rising more quickly.

Makes a 750g loaf

Basic Brown Bread

Strong brown bread flour is ground from the wholewheat kernel like wholemeal flour, but has some of the bran removed, so has a finer texture. It makes a better loaf when combined with a little white bread flour; the molasses or treacle enriches both the flavour and colour.

Ingredients:
1 tsp molasses or black treacle
350ml lukewarm water
25g butter, at room temperature
400g strong brown bread flour
100g strong white bread flour
1½ tsp salt
1 tsp caster sugar
1½ tsp fast-action dried yeast

- Lift the bread pan out of the bread machine and fit the kneading blade. Stir the molasses or black treacle into the water until blended, then pour into the pan. Add the butter, followed by the flours.
- Put the salt and sugar in separate corners of the pan, then make a shallow dip in the middle of the flour and add the yeast.
- Fit the pan into the bread machine, shut the lid and set to the wholewheat setting with a crust of your choice. Press start.
- After baking, lift the pan out of the machine using oven gloves. Carefully shake out the loaf to remove it from the pan, then transfer to a wire rack, standing the loaf on its base. Leave to cool.

Baker's tip
- If you don't have molasses or black treacle, add 1 tbsp dark or light soft brown sugar and leave out the caster sugar.

Quantities for a large (900g) loaf
1 tsp molasses or black treacle
420ml lukewarm water
30g butter, at room temperature
475g strong brown bread flour
125g strong white bread flour
1¾ tsp salt
1½ tsp caster sugar
1¾ tsp fast-action dried yeast

Quantities for a small (450g) loaf
½ tsp molasses or black treacle
210ml lukewarm water
15g butter, at room temperature
225g strong brown bread flour
75g strong white bread flour
¾ tsp salt
¾ tsp caster sugar
¾ tsp fast-action dried yeast

Soft Brown Bread

Ingredients:
325ml lukewarm water
2 tbsp sunflower oil
250g strong brown bread flour
2 tbsp skimmed milk powder
250g strong white bread flour
1½ tsp salt
1 tbsp soft light brown sugar
1½ tsp fast-action dried
   yeast

*Quantities for a large
   (900g) loaf*
390ml lukewarm water
2½ tbsp sunflower oil
300g strong brown bread flour
2½ tbsp skimmed milk
   powder
300g strong white bread flour
1¾ tsp salt
1½ tbsp soft light brown
   sugar
1¾ tsp fast-action dried
   yeast

*Quantities for a small
   (450g) loaf*
195ml lukewarm water
1¼ tbsp sunflower oil
150g strong brown bread flour
1¼ tbsp skimmed milk
   powder
150g strong white bread flour
¾ tsp salt
¾ tbsp soft light brown
   sugar
¾ tsp fast-action dried yeast

This simple brown loaf is made from half brown and half white flour and enriched with milk powder and sunflower oil, so it has a lighter colour and softer texture than a traditional brown loaf. It is ideal for those who enjoy the flavour of brown bread, but prefer the lighter texture of white.

- Lift the bread pan out of the bread machine and fit the kneading blade. Pour the water into the pan and add the oil. Add the strong brown bread flour, then sprinkle over the milk powder, followed by the white bread flour.
- Put the salt and sugar in separate corners of the pan, then make a shallow dip in the middle of the flour and add the yeast.
- Fit the pan into the bread machine, shut the lid and set to the basic white bread setting with a crust of your choice. Press start.
- After baking, lift the pan out of the machine using oven gloves. Carefully shake out the loaf to remove it from the pan, then transfer to a wire rack, standing the loaf on its base. Leave to cool.

Baker's tip
- Using skimmed milk powder allows you to use the timer delay setting, but if you are baking immediately, you can use 200ml milk and 125ml lukewarm water instead.

Speedy Seeded Bread

Many bread machines have a faster cycle, which usually takes half to two-thirds the time of the basic bread cycle to produce a baked loaf. The texture may be slightly closer but the loaf will still be well risen if you use warm water and add a little extra yeast to the mix.

- Lift the bread pan out of the bread machine and fit the kneading blade. Pour in the water, then add the oil, followed by about half of the flour. Sprinkle over the pumpkin and sunflower seeds, then add the rest of the flour.
- Put the salt and sugar in separate corners of the pan, then make a shallow dip in the middle of the flour and add the yeast.
- Fit the pan into the bread machine, shut the lid and set to the fast white setting with a crust of your choice. Press start.
- After baking, lift the pan out of the machine using oven gloves. Carefully shake out the loaf to remove it from the pan, then transfer to a wire rack, standing the loaf on its base. Leave to cool.

Baker's tip
- Once the packet is opened, store seeds in a sealed container in the fridge to keep them really fresh.

Ingredients:
325ml lukewarm water
2 tbsp sunflower oil
500g strong white bread
　flour
2 tbsp pumpkin seeds
2 tbsp sunflower seeds
1¼ tsp salt
1 tbsp caster sugar
2 tsp fast-action dried
　yeast

*Quantities for a large
　(900g) loaf*
390ml lukewarm water
2 tbsp sunflower oil
600g strong white bread
　flour
2½ tbsp pumpkin seeds
2½ tbsp sunflower seeds
1¼ tsp salt
4 tsp caster sugar
2½ tsp fast-action dried
　yeast

*Quantities for a small
　(450g) loaf*
195ml lukewarm water
1 tbsp sunflower oil
300g strong white bread
　flour
4 tsp pumpkin seeds
4 tsp sunflower seeds
¾ tsp salt
2 tsp caster sugar
1¼ tsp fast-action dried
　yeast

Rapid White Loaf

Ingredients:
300ml lukewarm water
2 tbsp sunflower oil
500g strong white bread
    flour
1 tsp salt
4 tsp caster sugar
1 tbsp fast-action dried
    yeast

*Quantities for a large
    (900g) loaf*
350ml lukewarm water
2 tbsp sunflower oil
600g strong white bread
    flour
1¼ tsp salt
5 tsp caster sugar
4 tsp fast-action dried yeast

*Quantities for a small
    (450g) loaf*
175ml lukewarm water
1 tbsp sunflower oil
300g strong white bread
    flour
¾ tsp salt
2½ tsp caster sugar
2 tsp fast-action dried yeast

This is for the extra-fast bread cycle on some machines that will produce a loaf in around an hour. The loaf may rise less, have a softer crust and be a little denser, but using lukewarm water, a little less salt and more yeast will help achieve the best results.

- Lift the bread pan out of the bread machine and fit the kneading blade. Pour in the water, then add the oil, followed by the flour.
- Put the salt and sugar in separate corners of the pan, then make a shallow dip in the middle of the flour and add the yeast.
- Fit the pan into the bread machine, shut the lid and set to the rapid setting with a crust of your choice. Press start.
- After baking, lift the pan out of the machine using oven gloves. Carefully shake out the loaf to remove it from the pan, then transfer to a wire rack, standing the loaf on its base.

Baker's tip
- The rapid (1 hour) setting is unsuitable for breads with a high proportion of brown or wholemeal flour.

Economy White Bread

Strong bread flour is used for bread-making because it is high in gluten; the substance which stretches the dough and traps air as it cooks. Ordinary plain flour contains less gluten, and on its own would make a close-textured, crumbly bread. You can, however, take advantage of 'economy' plain flour from the supermarket by mixing with strong bread flour to make an inexpensive loaf.

- Lift the bread pan out of the bread machine and fit the kneading blade. Pour in the water, then add the oil, followed by the flour.
- Put the salt and sugar in separate corners of the pan, then make a shallow dip in the middle of the flour and add the yeast.
- Fit the pan into the bread machine, shut the lid and set to the basic white setting with a crust of your choice. Press start.
- After baking, lift the pan out of the machine using oven gloves. Carefully shake out the loaf to remove it from the pan, then transfer to a wire rack, standing the loaf on its base. Leave to cool.

Ingredients:
325ml water
2 tbsp vegetable oil
300g strong white bread
    flour
200g plain white flour
1¼ tsp salt
1 tbsp caster sugar
1¼ tsp fast-action dried
    yeast

*Quantities for a large
    (900g) loaf*
390ml water
2 tbsp vegetable oil
350g strong white bread
    flour
250g plain white flour
1¾ tsp salt
4 tsp caster sugar
1¾ tsp fast-action dried
    yeast

*Quantities for a small
    (450g) loaf*
195ml water
1 tbsp vegetable oil
175g strong white bread
    flour
125g plain white flour
1 tsp salt
2 tsp caster sugar
1 tsp fast-action dried
    yeast

Classic Breads

This selection of recipes includes classic flours from around the world making breads with a wide variety of textures and flavours. Using grains other than wheat, you can create complex, hearty breads containing oats, rye and whole grains. Because most grains other than wheat have little or no gluten, many flours are combined with wheat flour. Traditional English blends, such as Granary and Malthouse, contain both wholemeal and white flour, together with malted wheat grains, and Barleycorn is a mixture of wheat and barley flour with malted barley flakes and linseeds. Rye flour is used in many rich and close-textured European breads such as Black bread and German dark rye bread. This chapter also features light and airy loaves such as French-style bread and includes old favourites like Farmhouse white bread and milk loaf.

CHAPTER 5

Farmhouse White Loaf

Ingredients:
325ml water
25g butter
500g strong white bread
  flour plus 1 tsp for
  dusting
2 tbsp skimmed milk powder
1 tsp salt
1 tbsp caster sugar
1 tsp fast-action dried yeast

*Quantities for a large
  (900g) loaf*
390ml water
30g butter
600g strong white bread
  flour plus 1 tsp for
  dusting
2½ tbsp skimmed milk
  powder
1¼ tsp salt
4 tsp caster sugar
1¼ tsp fast-action dried
  yeast

*Quantities for a small
  (450g) loaf*
195ml water
15g butter
300g strong white bread
  flour plus ½ tsp for
  dusting
1¼ tbsp skimmed milk
  powder
¾ tsp salt
2 tsp caster sugar
¾ tsp fast-action dried yeast

Milk powder gives this classic loaf a softer and more evenly textured crumb and crustier crust. A light dusting of flour is the traditional finish to this loaf; this can either be done before baking begins, or at the end when the loaf is still hot.

- Lift the bread pan out of the bread machine and fit the kneading blade. Pour in the water, then add the butter, followed by about half of the 500g flour. Sprinkle over the milk powder, followed by the rest of the flour.
- Put the salt and sugar in separate corners of the pan, then make a shallow dip in the middle and add the yeast.
- Fit the pan into the bread machine, shut the lid and set to the basic white setting with a light or medium crust (milk powder will make the crust slightly darker and crisper). Press start.
- After baking, lift the pan out of the machine using oven gloves. Carefully shake out the loaf to remove it from the pan, then transfer to a wire rack, standing the loaf on its base. Lightly dust the top with the remaining 1 tsp flour while the loaf is hot. Leave to cool.

Baker's tip
- Fresh milk can be used instead of the water and milk powder if preferred, providing you are not using the delayed time setting.

Milk Loaf

This classic loaf is enriched with milk, both semi-skimmed and a spoonful of skimmed milk powder. This gives it a soft, almost fluffy, even texture and a lightly floured, golden crust. It is perfect for serving thickly sliced and buttered with a fruity good-quality jam.

- Lift the bread pan out of the bread machine and fit the kneading blade. Pour in the semi-skimmed milk, then add the butter, followed by the 500g flour.
- Put the salt, skimmed milk powder and sugar in separate corners of the pan, then make a shallow dip in the middle of the flour and add the yeast.
- Fit the pan into the bread machine, shut the lid and set to the basic white setting with a light or medium crust. Press start.
- After baking, lift the pan out of the machine using oven gloves. Carefully shake out the loaf to remove it from the pan, then transfer to a wire rack, standing the loaf on its base.
- Lightly dust the top with the remaining flour while the loaf is hot. Leave to cool.

Baker's tips
- Use skimmed milk instead of semi-skimmed if preferred, or full-fat milk (in which case reduce the amount of butter by 5g).
- A medium crust setting will give a very golden crust, so choose the light setting if you prefer a softer one.

Ingredients:
325ml semi-skimmed milk
25g butter
500g plus 1 tsp strong
    white bread flour
1¼ tsp salt
1 tbsp skimmed milk
    powder
1 tbsp caster sugar
1¼ tsp fast-action dried
    yeast

*Quantities for a large
    (900g) loaf*
390ml semi-skimmed milk
30g butter
600g plus 1 tsp strong
    white bread flour
1½ tsp salt
4 tsp skimmed milk powder
4 tsp caster sugar
1½ tsp fast-action dried
    yeast

*Quantities for a small
    (450g) loaf*
195ml semi-skimmed milk
15g butter
300g plus ½ tsp strong
    white bread flour
¾ tsp salt
2 tsp skimmed milk powder
2 tsp caster sugar
¾ tsp fast-action dried
    yeast

Country Oatmeal Bread

Ingredients:
300ml water
25g butter
75g medium oatmeal plus
extra for sprinkling
375g strong white bread flour
50g strong wholemeal or
brown bread flour
1 tsp salt
2 tbsp clear honey
1 tsp fast-action dried yeast

Quantities for a large
(900g) loaf
360ml water
30g butter
90g medium oatmeal plus
extra for sprinkling
450g strong white bread flour
60g strong wholemeal or
brown bread flour
1¼ tsp salt
2 tbsp plus 1 tsp honey
1¼ tsp fast-action dried
yeast

Quantities for a small
(450g) loaf
180ml water
15g butter
45g medium oatmeal plus
extra for sprinkling
225g strong white bread flour
30g strong wholemeal or
brown bread flour
½ tsp salt
1 tbsp honey
¾ tsp fast-action dried yeast

The oatmeal makes this bread moister and the texture a little closer without being heavy. Honey sweetens and enhances the flavour and together they create a tasty breakfast bread, perfect for toasting and serving with creamy butter and an extra drizzle of fragrant honey.

- Lift the bread pan out of the bread machine and fit the kneading blade. Pour in the water, then add the butter, followed by the oatmeal and flours.
- Put the salt and honey in separate corners of the pan (but don't let the honey drizzle down the side of the pan as it may stick and burn), then make a shallow dip in the middle and add the yeast.
- Fit the pan into the bread machine, shut the lid and set to the basic white setting with a medium or dark crust. Press start.
- Just before baking, brush the top of the dough with water and sprinkle with the remaining oatmeal.
- After baking, lift the pan out of the machine using oven gloves. Carefully shake out the loaf to remove it from the pan, then transfer to a wire rack, standing the loaf on its base. Leave to cool.

Baker's tip
- If you don't have any oatmeal, blitz ordinary porridge oats in a food processor for a few seconds until coarsely ground and use instead.

Makes a 750g loaf

Soft-grain Bread

This is made with soft-grain bread flour: strong white bread flour with the addition of kibbled or cracked grains of wheat and rye which provide extra fibre, flavour and texture to the loaf, so it has the best of both white and wholemeal bread.

- Lift the bread pan out of the bread machine and fit the kneading blade. Pour in the water and milk, then add the oil, followed by the flour.
- Put the salt and honey in separate corners of the pan (making sure the honey doesn't touch the side), then make a shallow dip in the middle of the flour and add the yeast.
- Fit the pan into the bread machine, shut the lid and set to the basic white setting with a light or medium crust. Press start.
- After baking, lift the pan out of the machine using oven gloves. Carefully shake out the loaf to remove it from the pan, then transfer to a wire rack, standing the loaf on its base. Leave to cool.

Baker's tip
- Milk gives the loaf a slightly softer texture, but you can use all water if you prefer.

Ingredients:
225ml water
100ml skimmed or semi-skimmed milk
2 tbsp sunflower oil
500g soft-grain strong white bread flour
1¼ tsp salt
1 tbsp clear honey
1¼ tsp fast-action dried yeast

Quantities for a large (900g) loaf
270ml water
120ml milk
2½ tbsp sunflower oil
600g soft-grain strong white bread flour
1½ tsp salt
4 tsp clear honey
1½ tsp fast-action dried yeast.

Quantities for a small (450g) loaf
135ml water
4 tbsp/60ml skimmed or semi-skimmed milk
1 tbsp plus 1 tsp sunflower oil
300g soft-grain strong white bread flour
¾ tsp salt
2 tsp clear honey
¾ tsp fast-action dried yeast

Granary Loaf

The unique taste of Granary flour comes from malting the wheat, where partially germinated grains are slowly toasted to give a sweetness and slightly crunchy texture to the resulting bread. The flavour works well with both savoury and sweet accompaniments.

Ingredients:
350ml water
25g butter, at room temperature
500g Granary bread flour
1½ tsp salt
1 tbsp light soft brown sugar
1¼ tsp fast-action dried yeast

Quantities for a large (900g) loaf
400ml water
30g butter, at room temperature
600g Granary bread flour
1¾ tsp salt
4 tsp light soft brown sugar
1½ tsp fast-action dried yeast

Quantities for a small (450g) loaf
200ml water
15g butter, at room temperature
300g Granary bread flour
¾ tsp salt
2 tsp light soft brown sugar
¾ tsp fast-action dried yeast

- Lift the bread pan out of the bread machine and fit the kneading blade. Pour in the water, then add the butter, followed by the flour.
- Put the salt and sugar in separate corners of the pan, then make a shallow dip in the middle of the flour and add the yeast.
- Fit the pan into the bread machine, shut the lid and set to the wholewheat setting with a medium crust. Press start.
- After baking, lift the pan out of the machine using oven gloves. Carefully shake out the loaf to remove it from the pan, then transfer to a wire rack, standing the loaf on its base. Leave to cool.

Baker's tip
- Malthouse flour may be used instead of Granary bread flour, if preferred.

Quick Light Granary Loaf

Most bread machines have a rapid programme intended for white bread only, but a light-textured brown loaf can be achieved on this shorter cycle by using a blend of Granary and white bread flour, warm water and extra yeast to hasten the rising of the dough.

- Lift the bread pan out of the bread machine and fit the kneading blade. Pour in the water, then add the oil, followed by the flours.
- Put the salt and sugar in separate corners of the pan, then make a shallow dip in the middle of the flour and add the yeast.
- Fit the pan into the bread machine, shut the lid and set to the rapid white setting with a light crust. Press start.
- After baking, lift the pan out of the machine using oven gloves. Carefully shake out the loaf to remove it from the pan, then transfer to a wire rack, standing the loaf on its base. Leave to cool.

Baker's tip
- This is not suitable for making as a large loaf.

Ingredients:
300ml lukewarm water
2 tbsp sunflower oil
200g Granary bread flour
275g strong white bread
   flour
1½ tsp salt
1 tbsp dark soft brown
   sugar
2½ tsp fast-action dried
   yeast

*Quantities for a small
   (450g) loaf*
180ml lukewarm water
1 tbsp sunflower oil
120g Granary bread flour
165g strong white bread
   flour
¾ tsp salt
2 tsp dark soft brown sugar
1½ tsp fast-action dried
   yeast

Makes a 750g loaf

Malthouse Loaf

Ingredients:
1 tbsp malt extract
325ml lukewarm water
25g butter, at room
   temperature
500g Malthouse bread flour
1¼ tsp salt
1¼ tsp fast-action dried
   yeast

*Quantities for a large
   (900g) loaf*
4 tsp malt extract
390ml lukewarm water
30g butter
600g Malthouse bread flour
1½ tsp salt
1½ tsp fast-action dried
   yeast

*Quantities for a small
   (450g) loaf*
2 tsp malt extract
195ml lukewarm water
15g butter
300g Malthouse bread flour
¾ tsp salt
¾ tsp fast-action dried yeast

Like Granary flour, Malthouse flour is a blend of brown wheat flour and malted wheat flakes, but also has a small amount of rye and malt flour. It makes a lovely flavoursome light brown loaf, here with a little extra malt extract to intensify the flavour and colour.

- Lift the bread pan out of the bread machine and fit the kneading blade. Stir the malt extract into the water, then pour into the bread pan. Add the butter, followed by the flour.
- Put the salt and yeast in separate corners of the pan.
- Fit the pan into the bread machine, shut the lid and set to the wholewheat setting with a medium crust. Press start.
- After baking, lift the pan out of the machine using oven gloves. Carefully shake out the loaf to remove it from the pan, then transfer to a wire rack, standing the loaf on its base. Leave to cool.

Baker's tip
- If preferred, use 1 tbsp light soft brown sugar instead of the malt extract, adding it with the flour.

Barleycorn Bread

Barleycorn bread flour is a blend of wheat and barley flours combined with malted barley flakes and linseeds. It makes a lovely light brown loaf with all the taste and texture of bread that you can buy from delicatessens and wholefood stores.

- Lift the bread pan out of the bread machine and fit the kneading blade. Pour in the water, then add the oil, followed by the flour.
- Put the salt and sugar in separate corners of the pan, then make a shallow dip in the middle of the flour and add the yeast.
- Fit the pan into the bread machine, shut the lid and set to the wholewheat setting with a light or medium crust. Press start.
- After baking, lift the pan out of the machine using oven gloves. Carefully shake out the loaf to remove it from the pan, then transfer to a wire rack, standing the loaf on its base. Leave to cool.

Ingredients:
325ml lukewarm water
1 tbsp sunflower oil
500g Barleycorn flour
1 tsp salt
2 tsp caster sugar
1¼ tsp fast-action dried yeast

Quantities for a large (900g) loaf
390ml lukewarm water
4 tsp sunflower oil
600g Barleycorn flour
1¼ tsp salt
2½ tsp caster sugar
1½ tsp fast-action dried yeast

Quantities for a small (450g) loaf
195ml lukewarm water
2 tsp sunflower oil
300g Barleycorn flour
¾ tsp salt
1¼ tsp caster sugar
¾ tsp fast-action dried yeast

Multi-grain Loaf

Ingredients:
350ml lukewarm water
2 tbsp sunflower oil
100g strong wholemeal or brown bread flour
3 tbsp wheat flakes or porridge oats
2 tbsp mixed seeds such as pumpkin, sunflower, sesame or linseeds
25g millet
25g bulghar wheat
300g strong white bread flour
1¼ tsp salt
1 tbsp golden caster sugar
1½ tsp fast-action dried yeast

Although you can buy multi-grain bread flour, this recipe uses white and wholemeal bread flours, plus a mixture of different seeds and cereals. You can create your own blend and substitute one type, but don't be tempted to use more than suggested here.

- Lift the bread pan out of the bread machine and fit the kneading blade. Pour in the water, then add the oil, followed by the wholemeal or brown bread flour. Sprinkle the wheat flakes or oats, seeds, millet and bulghar wheat over, then add the white bread flour.
- Put the salt and sugar in separate corners of the pan, then make a shallow dip in the middle of the flour and add the yeast.
- Fit the pan into the bread machine, shut the lid and set to the multi-grain or wholewheat setting with the crust of your choice. Press start.
- After baking, lift the pan out of the machine using oven gloves. Carefully shake out the loaf to remove it from the pan, then transfer to a wire rack, standing the loaf on its base.
- Lightly dust the top with the remaining flour while the loaf is hot. Leave to cool.

Quantities for a large (900g) loaf
425ml warm water
2 tbsp sunflower oil
125g strong wholemeal or brown bread flour
3½ tbsp wheat flakes or oats
2½ tbsp mixed seeds, such as sunflower, pumpkin and sesame seeds
30g millet
30g bulghar wheat
350g strong white bread flour
1½ tsp salt
4 tsp sugar
1¾ tsp yeast

Quantities for a small (450g) loaf
215ml warm water
1 tbsp sunflower oil
60g strong wholemeal or brown bread flour
1½ tbsp wheat flakes or oats
1 tbsp mixed seeds, such as sunflower, pumpkin and sesame seeds
15g millet
15g bulghar wheat
175g strong white bread flour
¾ tsp salt
2 tsp sugar
¾ tsp yeast

Makes a 750g loaf

Boston Brown Bread

Created by American settlers in the days before most homes had ovens, Boston bread was originally steamed rather than baked in a tall, round container, usually a huge coffee tin. This version is much simpler to make and has all the traditional flavour and close texture.

- Put the buttermilk and molasses in a small pan and heat, stirring, until barely warm.
- Lift the bread pan out of the bread machine and fit the kneading blade. Pour in the buttermilk and molasses mixture. Add the brown bread flour, rye flour, cornmeal and white bread flour.
- Put the salt and yeast in separate corners of the pan.
- Put the raisins in the automatic dispenser if your machine has one. Fit the pan into the bread machine, shut the lid and set to the multi-grain or wholewheat setting with a light crust. Press start.
- If you don't have an automatic dispenser, add the raisins when the machine beeps or halfway through the kneading cycle.
- After baking, lift the pan out of the machine using oven gloves. Carefully shake out the loaf to remove it from the pan, then transfer to a wire rack, standing the loaf on its base. Leave to cool.

Baker's tips
- Buttermilk is typically used in this bread, but if you prefer you can use 250ml semi-skimmed milk and ½ tsp lemon juice instead.
- This is not suitable for making as a larger loaf.

Ingredients:
250ml buttermilk
6 tbsp molasses
150g strong brown bread flour
50g rye flour
50g cornmeal or fine polenta
175g strong white bread flour
1½ tsp salt
1¼ tsp fast-action dried yeast
75g raisins

Quantities for a small (450g) loaf
150ml buttermilk
3½ tbsp molasses
90g strong brown bread flour
30g rye flour
30g cornmeal or fine polenta
100g strong white bread flour
¾ tsp salt
¾ tsp fast-action dried yeast
45g raisins

Light Rye and Caraway Loaf

Ingredients:
350ml warm water
1 tbsp plain yoghurt
2 tbsp sunflower oil
150g rye flour
1 tbsp skimmed milk powder
1 tbsp caraway seeds plus
    extra for sprinkling
350g strong white bread
    flour
1½ tsp salt
1½ tbsp soft light brown
    sugar
1½ tsp fast-action dried
    yeast

*Quantities for a large
    (900g) loaf*
420ml warm water
4 tsp plain yoghurt
2 tbsp plus 1 tsp sunflower
    oil
180g rye flour
4 tsp skimmed milk powder
4 tsp caraway seeds plus
    extra for sprinkling
420g strong white bread
    flour
1¾ tsp salt
5 tsp soft light brown sugar
1¾ tsp fast-action dried
    yeast

This is a New York-style rye loaf with a light texture and slightly craggy, rustic look. Rye flour is low in gluten, so rye breads won't rise as much as other machine-made breads, but by combining it with strong white flour you should still achieve a reasonable volume.

- Lift the bread pan out of the bread machine and fit the kneading blade. Pour in the water, then add the yoghurt and oil, followed by the rye flour. Sprinkle over the milk powder and caraway seeds, then add the white bread flour.
- Put the salt and sugar in separate corners of the pan, then make a shallow dip in the middle of the flour and add the yeast.
- Fit the pan into the bread machine, shut the lid and set to the multi-grain or wholewheat setting with a light or medium crust. Press start.
- When the loaf starts to bake, brush the top with water and sprinkle with the extra caraway seeds.
- After baking, lift the pan out of the machine using oven gloves. Carefully shake out the loaf to remove it from the pan, then transfer to a wire rack, standing the loaf on its base. Leave to cool.

Baker's tip
- If you like, you can add the caraway seeds at the beginning of mixing and not in the automatic dispenser or part-way through the cycle, to enable their flavour to permeate throughout the bread.

Quantities for a small (450g) loaf
210ml warm water
2 tsp plain yoghurt
4 tsp sunflower oil
90g rye flour
2 tsp skimmed milk
    powder

2 tsp caraway seeds plus extra for
    sprinkling
210g strong white bread flour
¾ tsp salt
2½ tsp soft light brown sugar
¾ tsp fast-action dried yeast

German Dark Rye Bread

Rye flour has a typically north European, tangy flavour. This bread is not quite as dark, dense and rich as pumpernickel, but has similar flavourings. Serve it thinly sliced and spread with butter, or it is equally good topped with cream cheese, smoked salmon and fresh dill.

Ingredients:
350ml lukewarm water
1 tbsp molasses or black treacle
1 tsp lemon juice
25g butter, at room temperature
250g rye flour
1 tbsp caraway seeds
250g very strong white bread flour
1½ tsp salt
1½ tsp soft light brown sugar
1½ tsp fast-action dried yeast

- Lift the bread pan out of the bread machine and fit the kneading blade. Stir the molasses or treacle and lemon juice into the water until the blended, then pour into the bread pan. Add the butter, followed by the rye flour, caraway seeds and white bread flour.
- Put the salt and sugar in separate corners of the pan, then make a shallow dip in the middle of the flour and add the yeast.
- Fit the pan into the bread machine, shut the lid and set to the multi-grain or wholewheat setting with a light or medium crust. Press start.
- After baking, lift the pan out of the machine using oven gloves. Carefully shake out the loaf to remove it from the pan, then transfer to a wire rack, standing the loaf on its base.
- Leave to cool.

Quantities for a large (900g) loaf
420ml lukewarm water
4 tsp molasses or black treacle
1 tsp lemon juice
30g butter, at room temperature
300g rye flour
4 tsp caraway seeds
300g strong white bread flour
1¾ tsp salt
1¾ tsp soft light brown sugar
1½ tsp fast-action dried yeast

Quantities for a small (450g) loaf
210ml lukewarm water
2 tsp molasses or black treacle
½ tsp lemon juice
15g butter, at room temperature
150g rye flour
2 tsp caraway seeds
150g strong white bread flour
¾ tsp salt
¾ tsp soft light brown sugar
¾ tsp fast-action dried yeast

Black Bread

Ingredients:
325ml lukewarm water
2 tbsp molasses or black
  treacle
2 tsp cider vinegar
2 tsp instant coffee granules
25g butter, at room
  temperature
350g very strong white
  bread flour
150g rye flour
2 tbsp unsweetened cocoa
  powder
1½ tsp salt
1¼ tsp fast-action dried
  yeast

Often known as Russian black bread, like many European rye loaves, it includes cocoa and coffee to darken the colour although the taste of these is barely perceptible in the finished product. Close-textured, it is good thinly sliced with pâtés and strong-flavoured cheeses.

- Lift the bread pan out of the bread machine and fit the kneading blade. Stir the molasses, vinegar and coffee granules into the water until dissolved. Pour into the pan, then add the butter, followed by the flours and the cocoa.
- Put the salt and yeast in separate corners of the pan.
- Fit the pan into the bread machine, shut the lid and set to the basic white setting with a medium crust. Press start.
- After baking, lift the pan out of the machine using oven gloves. Carefully shake out the loaf to remove it from the pan, then transfer to a wire rack, standing the loaf on its base. Leave to cool.

Baker's tip
- Balsamic vinegar or lemon juice may be used instead of the cider vinegar, if preferred.

Quantities for a large (900g) loaf
400ml lukewarm water
2 tbsp plus 1 tsp molasses or black
  treacle
2 tsp cider vinegar
2 tsp instant coffee granules
30g butter
420g very strong white bread flour
180g rye flour
2 tbsp unsweetened cocoa powder
1¾ tsp salt
1¼ tsp fast-action dried yeast

Quantities for a small (450g) loaf
200ml lukewarm water
1 tbsp molasses or black treacle
1 tsp cider vinegar
1 tsp instant coffee granules
15g butter
110g very strong white bread flour
90g rye flour
1 tbsp unsweetened cocoa powder
¾ tsp salt
¾ tsp fast-action dried yeast

Makes a 1kg loaf

Sourdough Loaf

This is a basic white loaf with the unique flavour that comes from using a sourdough starter – the traditional method of leavening bread without yeast. You'll need to plan several days in advance and follow the method for this on page 23.

- Lift the bread pan out of the bread machine and fit the kneading blade. Pour in the starter and water, then add the butter followed by the 500g flour.
- Put the salt and sugar in separate corners of the pan, then make a shallow dip in the middle of the flour and add the yeast.
- Fit the pan into the bread machine, shut the lid and set to the basic white setting with the crust of your choice. Press start.
- After baking, lift the pan out of the machine using oven gloves. Carefully shake out the loaf to remove it from the pan, then transfer to a wire rack, standing the loaf on its base.
- Lightly dust the top with the remaining 1 tsp flour while the loaf is hot. Leave to cool.

Ingredients:
300ml sourdough starter (see page 23)
175ml lukewarm water
25g butter, at room temperature
500g plus 1 tsp very strong white bread flour
1½ tsp salt
1 tbsp golden caster sugar

Quantities for a small (500g) loaf
150ml sourdough starter
90ml lukewarm water
15g butter, at room temperature
250g plus ½ tsp very strong white bread flour
¾ tsp salt
1½ tsp golden caster sugar

Anadama Bread

Ingredients:
300ml lukewarm water
3 tbsp molasses
1 tsp lemon juice
25g butter
50g rye flour
50g cornmeal or polenta
400g very strong white
  bread flour
1½ tsp salt
1¼ tsp fast-action dried
  yeast

A traditional dark-coloured bread from New England, this is made with white flour, rye flour and cornmeal, enriched and sweetened with molasses. The texture is dense, grainy and slightly chewy – great eaten fresh and warm or thickly sliced and lightly toasted.

- Lift the bread pan out of the bread machine and fit the kneading blade. Stir the molasses and lemon juice into the water until blended, then pour into the bread pan. Add the butter, followed by the rye flour, cornmeal or polenta and white bread flour.
- Put the salt in a corner of the pan, then make a shallow dip in the middle of the flour and add the yeast.
- Fit the pan into the bread machine, shut the lid and set to the basic white setting with a light or medium crust. Press start.
- After baking, lift the pan out of the machine using oven gloves. Carefully shake out the loaf to remove it from the pan, then transfer to a wire rack, standing the loaf on its base. Leave to cool.

Quantities for a large (900g) loaf
360ml lukewarm water
4 tbsp molasses
1 tsp lemon juice
30g butter
60g rye flour
60g cornmeal or polenta
480g very strong white bread flour
1¾ tsp salt
1¼ tsp fast-action dried yeast

Quantities for a small (450g) loaf
180ml lukewarm water
2 tbsp molasses
½ tsp lemon juice
15g butter
30g rye flour
30g cornmeal or polenta
240g very strong white bread flour
¾ tsp salt
¾ tsp fast-action dried yeast

French-style Bread

Many machines have a French bread programme designed for recipes with little or no sugar and fat, which therefore need longer rising times and a higher baking temperature. French-milled flour gives the best results, but you can use unbleached white bread flour.

- Lift the bread pan out of the bread machine and fit the kneading blade. Pour in the water, then add the flour.
- Put the salt and sugar in separate corners of the pan, then make a shallow dip in the middle of the flour and add the yeast.
- Fit the pan into the bread machine, shut the lid and set to the French bread setting with the crust of your choice. Press start.
- After baking, lift the pan out of the machine using oven gloves. Carefully shake out the loaf to remove it from the pan, then transfer to a wire rack, standing the loaf on its base.
- Leave to cool.

Ingredients:
300ml water
475g Type 55 French flour
1 tsp salt
1 tsp caster sugar
1 tsp fast-action dried
    yeast

*Quantities for a large
    (900g) loaf*
360ml water
570g Type 55 French flour
1¼ tsp salt
1¼ tsp caster sugar
1¼ tsp fast-action dried
    yeast

*Quantities for a small
    (450g) loaf*
180ml water
285g Type 55 French flour
¾ tsp salt
¾ tsp caster sugar
¾ tsp fast-action dried
    yeast

Savoury Enriched Breads

CHAPTER

6

All manner of savoury flavouring ingredients can be added to bread-machine loaves. Perhaps the most obvious choices are fresh and dried herbs, grated and crumbled cheeses, caramelised onions, olives and sun-dried tomatoes. Classic food combinations such as Cheshire cheese and apple, celery and walnut, smoky bacon and maple syrup, hot potato and horseradish all work well in bread, but if you are looking for vibrant colours, interesting tastes and textures and perhaps something a little bit different, try adding vegetable purées or juices to make loaves such as sweet potato or beetroot bread, which has a lovely earthy flavour and vibrant pink hue.

You can also enrich bread with ingredients such as buttermilk, yoghurt and milk to give different tastes and textures. Try beer bread, made with stout for a rich, dark colour and distinctive flavour, or brown buttermilk bread, a lovely soft country-style loaf.

Finally, many recipes in this chapter suggest that if your machine doesn't have an automatic dispenser, you can add additional ingredients halfway through the kneading time. This prevents them being broken into smaller pieces and reduces wear and tear on your bread pan, but for totally effortless bread-making, you can add all the ingredients at the start of mixing if you prefer.

Savoury Enriched Breads • 65

Makes a 750g loaf

Brown Buttermilk Bread

Ingredients:
300ml buttermilk
2 tbsp water
20g butter, at room
   temperature
1 tbsp clear honey
400g strong brown bread flour
100g strong white bread
   flour
1 tsp salt
1¼ tsp fast-action dried
   yeast

*Quantities for a large
   (900g) loaf*
360ml buttermilk
2½ tbsp water
25g butter, at room
   temperature
4 tsp clear honey
475g strong brown bread flour
125g strong white bread
   flour
1¼ tsp salt
1½ tsp fast-action dried
   yeast

*Quantities for a small
   (375g) loaf*
150ml buttermilk
4 tsp water
10g butter, at room
   temperature
1½ tsp clear honey
200g strong brown bread flour
50g strong white bread flour
½ tsp salt
¾ tsp fast-action dried yeast

Contrary to its name, buttermilk is very low in fat. It is often used as a raising ingredient in yeast-free quick breads. Here it gives a rich flavour and a lovely light texture to the bread. Using a small amount of white flour makes a softer loaf, but you can use all brown flour.

- Lift the bread pan out of the bread machine and fit the kneading blade. Pour in the buttermilk and water, add the butter and honey, then the flour.
- Put the salt in one of the corners of the pan, then make a shallow dip in the middle of the flour and add the yeast.
- Fit the pan into the bread machine, shut the lid and set to the wholewheat setting with a crust of your choice. Press start.
- After baking, lift the pan out of the machine using oven gloves. Carefully shake out the loaf to remove it from the pan, then transfer to a wire rack, standing the loaf on its base. Leave to cool.

Baker's tip
- Buttermilk is traditionally the liquid left after the cream of the milk has been turned into butter by churning. Nowadays, it is usually made by adding a culture to skimmed milk. Try to remove it from the fridge about an hour before you need it, so that it is at room temperature. If you can't find buttermilk, stir 1 tsp lemon juice into skimmed milk and leave it to stand for a few minutes before using.

Malted Barley Bread

Barley flour has a lovely sweet and nutty flavour and dark, creamy colour. Because of its low gluten content, it needs to be blended with strong bread flour to make a well-risen loaf. You could use half white and half brown instead of all white for a more rustic bread.

- Lift the bread pan out of the bread machine and fit the kneading blade. Whisk the egg and malt extract together in a jug, then stir in the milk. Add enough water to make up the quantity of liquid to 350ml. Pour into the bread pan and add the butter.
- Add the white bread flour and barley flour. Put the salt in a corner of the pan, then make a shallow dip in the middle of the flour and add the yeast.
- Fit the pan into the bread machine, shut the lid and set to the basic white setting with a crust of your choice. Press start.
- After baking, lift the pan out of the machine using oven gloves. Carefully shake out the loaf to remove it from the pan, then transfer to a wire rack, standing the loaf on its base. Leave to cool.

Ingredients:
1 medium egg
1 tbsp malt extract
150ml skimmed milk
Water
25g butter, at room temperature
400g strong white bread flour
100g barley flour
1 tsp salt
1¼ tsp fast-action dried yeast

Quantities for a large (900g) loaf
1 large egg
4 tsp malt extract
180ml skimmed milk
Water to make up the quantity of liquid to 420ml
30g butter, at room temperature
480g strong white bread flour
120g barley flour
1¼ tsp salt
1¼ tsp fast-action dried yeast

Quantities for a small (450g) loaf
1 small egg
2 tsp malt extract
90ml skimmed milk
Water to make up the quantity of liquid to 240ml
15g butter, at room temperature
240g strong white bread flour
60g barley flour
¾ tsp salt
¾ tsp fast-action dried yeast

Makes a 750g loaf

Seeded Spelt Loaf

Ingredients:
75g mixed seeds, such as
    sunflower, pumpkin and
    sesame seeds
300ml lukewarm water
2 tbsp sunflower oil
200g white spelt flour
200g wholegrain spelt flour
100g strong white bread
    flour
1 tsp salt
1 tbsp golden caster sugar
1¼ tsp fast-action dried
    yeast

This is one of my favourite breads. It has the rich, nutty flavour of both white and wholegrain spelt flours but the lighter texture of white bread and a generous amount of toasted seeds. It's especially good eaten when freshly made, but also makes excellent toast.

- Put the seeds in a small non-stick frying pan and toast over a low heat for 3–4 minutes, stirring frequently, until they release a nutty aroma (take care not to allow them to burn). Remove the pan from the heat.
- Lift the bread pan out of the bread machine and fit the kneading blade. Pour the water into the bread pan and add the oil. Add all the flours. Put the salt and sugar in separate corners of the pan, then make a shallow dip in the middle of the flour and add the yeast.
- Put the toasted seeds in the automatic dispenser if your machine has one.
- Fit the pan into the bread machine, shut the lid and set to the basic white setting with a crust of your choice. Press start.
- If your machine doesn't have an automatic dispenser, add the seeds when the machine beeps or halfway through the kneading time.
- After baking, lift the pan out of the machine using oven gloves. Carefully shake out the loaf to remove it from the pan, then transfer to a wire rack, standing the loaf on its base. Leave to cool.

Quantities for a large (900g) loaf
90g mixed seeds, such as sunflower,
    pumpkin and sesame seeds
360ml lukewarm water
2 tbsp sunflower oil
240g white spelt flour
240g wholegrain spelt flour
120g strong white bread flour
1¼ tsp salt
4 tsp golden caster sugar
1½ tsp fast-action dried yeast

Quantities for a small (450g) loaf
45g mixed seeds, such as sunflower,
    pumpkin and sesame seeds
180ml lukewarm water
1 tbsp sunflower oil
120g white spelt flour
120g wholegrain spelt flour
60g strong white bread flour
¾ tsp salt
2 tsp golden caster sugar
¾ tsp fast-action dried yeast

Golden Cornmeal Bread

Cornmeal (sometimes called maize meal or maize flour) gives this loaf an attractive golden colour and a light, almost cake-like texture. It is very popular in the southern states of America and is perfect for serving with spicy bean-based dishes like chilli con carne.

- Lift the bread pan out of the bread machine and fit the kneading blade. Pour in the milk and water, then add the butter, followed by the flour and cornmeal.
- Put the salt and sugar in separate corners of the pan, then make a shallow dip in the middle of the cornmeal and add the yeast.
- Fit the pan into the bread machine, shut the lid and set to the basic white setting with a light or medium crust. Press start.
- Just before baking starts, brush the top of the dough with water and lightly sprinkle with cornmeal.
- After baking, lift the pan out of the machine using oven gloves. Carefully shake out the loaf to remove it from the pan, then transfer to a wire rack, standing the loaf on its base. Leave to cool.

Baker's tip
- Polenta is very similar to cornmeal and can be substituted, but make sure you choose fine or medium and not coarse polenta.

Ingredients:
150ml semi-skimmed milk
150ml lukewarm water
25g butter, at room temperature
350g strong white bread flour
150g cornmeal plus extra for sprinkling
1 tsp salt
1½ tbsp golden caster sugar
1 tsp fast-action dried yeast

Quantities for a large (900g) loaf
180ml semi-skimmed milk
180ml lukewarm water
30g butter
420g strong white bread flour
180g cornmeal
1¼ tsp salt
2 tbsp golden caster sugar
1¼ tsp fast-action dried yeast

Quantities for a small (450g) loaf
90ml semi-skimmed milk
90ml warm water
15g butter
210g strong white bread flour
90g cornmeal
¾ tsp salt
1 tbsp golden caster sugar
¾ tsp fast-action dried yeast

Buckwheat Brown Bread

Ingredients:
325ml lukewarm water
25g butter, at room
   temperature
425g strong brown bread
   flour
75g buckwheat flour
1¼ tsp salt
2 tsp caster sugar
1½ tsp fast-action dried
   yeast

*Quantities for a large
   (900g) loaf*
390ml lukewarm water
30g butter
500g strong brown bread
   flour
100g buckwheat flour
1½ tsp salt
2½ tsp caster sugar
1½ tsp fast-action dried
   yeast

*Quantities for a small
   (450g) loaf*
195ml lukewarm water
15g butter
250g strong brown bread
   flour
50g buckwheat
¾ tsp salt
1 tsp caster sugar
¾ tsp fast-action dried yeast

Just a small amount of buckwheat adds a lovely, nutty flavour and texture to bread, but because it is gluten-free it needs to be combined with strong bread flour to make a well-risen loaf. Here it works its magic with brown bread flour to make really tasty bread.

- Lift the bread pan out of the bread machine and fit the kneading blade. Pour the water into the pan, then add the butter, followed by the flours.
- Put the salt and sugar in separate corners of the pan, then make a shallow dip in the middle of the flour and add the yeast.
- Fit the pan into the bread machine, shut the lid and set to the wholewheat setting with a crust of your choice. Press start.
- After baking, lift the pan out of the machine using oven gloves. Carefully shake out the loaf to remove it from the pan, then transfer to a wire rack, standing the loaf on its base. Leave to cool.

Makes a 750g loaf

Toasted Seed Loaf

Seeds are full of nutritional goodness and toasting them brings out their delicious flavour. Most supermarkets sell packets of toasted seed mix, usually a combination of pumpkin, sunflower and sesame seeds and sometimes tiny linseeds as well.

- Lift the bread pan out of the bread machine and fit the kneading blade. Pour in the water, then add the oil, followed by the white and wholemeal bread flours.
- Put the salt and sugar in separate corners of the pan, then make a shallow dip in the middle of the flour and add the yeast.
- Put the seeds in the automatic dispenser if your machine has one.
- Fit the pan into the bread machine, shut the lid and set to the basic white setting with a light crust. Press start.
- If your machine doesn't have an automatic dispenser, add the seeds when the machine beeps or halfway through the kneading time.
- After baking, lift the pan out of the machine using oven gloves. Carefully shake out the loaf to remove it from the pan, then transfer to a wire rack, standing the loaf on its base. Leave to cool.

Baker's tip
- If you can't find toasted seed mix, you can easily make your own. Tip the seeds into a small non-stick frying pan and cook over a low heat for 3–4 minutes, stirring or shaking the pan frequently until the seeds smell very aromatic. Remove the pan from the heat before they start to colour as they will continue to cook in the residual heat for a minute or two.

Ingredients:
325ml water
2 tbsp sunflower oil
400g strong white bread flour
100g strong wholemeal bread flour
1 tsp salt
1 tablespoon soft light brown sugar
50g toasted seed mix
1 tsp fast-action dried yeast

Quantities for a large (900g) loaf
390ml water
2 tbsp sunflower oil
480g strong white bread flour
120g strong wholemeal bread flour
1¼ tsp salt
4 tsp soft light brown sugar
60g toasted seed mix
1¼ tsp fast-action dried yeast

Quantities for a small (450g) loaf
195ml water
1 tbsp sunflower oil
240g strong white bread flour
60g strong wholemeal bread flour
¾ tsp salt
2 tsp soft light brown sugar
30g toasted seed mix
¾ tsp fast-action dried yeast

Beer Bread

Ingredients:
150ml stout, Guinness or
   brown ale
150ml water
2 tbsp sunflower oil
475g Malthouse flour
1 tsp salt
1 tbsp light muscovado
   sugar
1¼ tsp fast-action dried
   yeast
1 tbsp poppy seeds

*Quantities for a large
  (900g) loaf*
180ml stout, Guinness or
   brown beer
180ml water
2 tbsp sunflower oil
570g Malthouse flour
1¼ tsp salt
4 tsp light muscovado sugar
1½ tsp fast-action dried
   yeast
4 tsp poppy seeds

*Quantities for a small
  (450g) loaf*
90ml stout, Guinness or
   brown beer
90ml water
1 tbsp sunflower oil
285g Malthouse flour
¾ tsp salt
2 tsp light muscovado sugar
¾ tsp fast-action dried yeast
2 tsp poppy seeds

A dark, rustic-style loaf made with Malthouse flour, with added depth from the stout or Guinness – the alcohol evaporates as the loaf bakes. It is lovely served slightly warm with cheese and pickles and perhaps a glass of the remaining stout.

- Lift the bread pan out of the bread machine and fit the kneading blade. Pour in the beer and water, then add the oil, followed by the flour.
- Put the salt and sugar in separate corners of the pan, then make a shallow dip in the middle of the flour and add the yeast.
- Put the poppy seeds in the automatic dispenser if your machine has one.
- Fit the pan into the bread machine, shut the lid and set to the wholewheat setting with a light crust. Press start.
- If your machine doesn't have an automatic dispenser, add the poppy seeds when the machine beeps or halfway through the kneading time.
- After baking, lift the pan out of the machine using oven gloves. Carefully shake out the loaf to remove it from the pan, then transfer to a wire rack, standing the loaf on its base. Leave to cool.

Semolina and Olive Oil Bread

Semolina is a coarse pale-yellow flour ground from hard durum wheat. In much of North Africa it is made into the staple, couscous, but is also used in bread-making. This loaf contains a high proportion of olive oil, which adds both flavour and moistness.

- Lift the bread pan out of the bread machine and fit the kneading blade. Pour in the water, then add the oil, followed by the semolina, white bread flour and sesame seeds.
- Put the salt and sugar in separate corners of the pan, then make a shallow dip in the middle of the flour and add the yeast.
- Fit the pan into the bread machine, shut the lid and set to the basic white setting with a light crust. Press start.
- After baking, lift the pan out of the machine using oven gloves. Carefully shake out the loaf to remove it from the pan, then transfer to a wire rack, standing the loaf on its base. Leave to cool.

Baker's tips
- Traditionally, this loaf would be shaped into a large, flattish round. If you prefer, make the dough in the bread machine, on the dough setting, then shape into a 20cm round on a lightly greased baking sheet. Cover with oiled clingfilm and allow to rise until doubled in size. Brush with egg glaze or milk and sprinkle with extra sesame seeds, then bake in a preheated oven at 200°C/gas 6 for 25 minutes.
- This is not suitable for making as a larger loaf.

Ingredients:
240ml water
4 tbsp olive oil
100g finely ground semolina or semolina flour
350g strong white bread flour
1 tbsp sesame seeds
1 tsp salt
2 tsp caster sugar
1¼ tsp fast-action dried yeast

Quantities for a small (450g) loaf
145ml water
2½ tbsp olive oil
60g finely ground semolina or semolina flour
210g strong white bread flour
¾ tsp salt
1½ tsp caster sugar
¾ tsp fast-action dried yeast

Makes a 900g loaf

Olive and Thyme Sourdough Bread

Ingredients:
300ml sourdough starter
(see page 23)
150ml lukewarm water
2 tbsp olive oil
500g very strong white
bread flour
2 tbsp fresh thyme leaves or
2 tsp dried thyme
1 tsp salt
2 tsp caster sugar
50g dry-packed black olives,
stoned and roughly
chopped

*Quantities for a small
(450g) loaf*
150ml sourdough starter
75ml lukewarm water
1 tbsp olive oil
250g very strong white
bread flour
1 tbsp fresh thyme or 1 tsp
dried thyme
½ tsp salt
1 tsp caster sugar
25g dry-packed olives,
stoned and roughly
chopped

This bread uses the sourdough starter on page 23. It is a wonderfully aromatic bread, studded with black olives and flavoured with olive oil and thyme. Slice thinly and serve with an extra drizzle of olive oil – perfect with a glass of wine on a summer evening.

- Lift the bread pan out of the bread machine and fit the kneading blade. Pour in the sourdough starter and water, then add the oil followed by about half the flour. Sprinkle over the thyme, then add the rest of the flour.
- Put the salt and sugar in separate corners of the pan.
- Put the olives in the automatic dispenser if you have one.
- Fit the pan into the bread machine, shut the lid and set to basic white setting with a medium crust. Press start.
- If you don't have an automatic dispenser, add the olives when the machine bleeps or halfway through the kneading time.
- After baking, lift the pan out of the machine using oven gloves. Carefully shake out the loaf to remove it from the pan, then transfer to a wire rack, standing the loaf on its base. Leave to cool.

Baker's tip
- To strip thyme leaves from their woody stems, hold a stalk at the top and then firmly run the forefinger and thumb of your other hand along the stalk from top to bottom.

Mixed Olive Bread

Extra olive oil gives this bread a softer crust and lovely flavour. Choose good-quality olives, preferably those in herb or spice-flavoured oil. For extra flavour, use some of the oil from the olives instead of the some of the olive oil.

- Lift the bread pan out of the bread machine and fit the kneading blade. Pour the water into the pan, then add the oil, followed by the flour.
- Put the salt and sugar in separate corners of the pan, then make a shallow dip in the middle of the flour and add the yeast.
- Put the olives in the automatic dispenser if you have one.
- Fit the pan into the bread machine, shut the lid and set to the basic white setting with a crust of your choice. Press start.
- If you don't have an automatic dispenser, add the olives when the machine bleeps or halfway through kneading time.
- After baking, lift the pan out of the machine using oven gloves. Carefully shake out the loaf to remove it from the pan, then transfer to a wire rack, standing the loaf on its base. Leave to cool.

Baker's tips
- Taste the olives before you bake; if they are very salty you may wish to add a little less salt to the bread dough.
- This is not suitable for making as a larger loaf.

Ingredients:
325ml water
3 tbsp virgin olive oil
500g strong white bread flour
1 tsp salt
2 tsp caster sugar
1 tsp fast-action dried yeast
100g black and green pitted olives, roughly chopped

Quantities for a small (425g) loaf
160ml water
1½ tbsp olive oil
250g strong white bread flour
½ tsp salt
1 tsp caster sugar
¾ tsp fast-action dried yeast
50g black and green pitted olives

Country Cheshire Cheese and Apple Bread

Ingredients:
20g unsalted butter
2 eating apples, peeled,
  cored and cut into 1cm
  chunks
1 tbsp golden caster sugar
275ml water
450g soft-grain bread flour
1 tsp salt
1 tsp fast-action dried yeast
75g Cheshire cheese, cut or
  crumbled into 1cm pieces

*Quantities for a small
  (450g) loaf*
15g unsalted butter
1 large eating apple
2 tsp golden caster sugar
165g soft-grain bread flour
¾ tsp salt
¾ tsp fast-action dried yeast
45g Cheshire cheese

In this country-style bread, sweet apples are the perfect partner for the creamy and slightly sharp flavour of Cheshire cheese. This recipe uses eating apples as they hold their shape as they are gently caramelised in a little butter.

- Heat the butter in a non-stick frying pan until melted. Add the apple and stir to coat in the butter, then cover with a lid and cook over a low heat for 3–4 minutes. Uncover and cook for a further 2 minutes, stirring frequently, until any excess moisture has evaporated. Sprinkle over the sugar, turn up the heat a little and cook, stirring, until the apples just start to caramelise and colour. Turn off the heat and leave to cool for a few minutes.
- Lift the bread pan out of the bread machine and fit the kneading blade. Tip the hot apple mixture into the pan and pour over the water. Add the flour, then put the salt and yeast in separate corners of the pan.
- Put the cheese in the automatic dispenser if you have one.
- Fit the pan into the bread machine, shut the lid and set to the basic white setting with a medium crust. Press start.
- If you don't have an automatic dispenser, add the cheese when the machine bleeps or halfway through the kneading time.
- After baking, lift the pan out of the machine using oven gloves. Carefully shake out the loaf to remove it from the pan, then transfer to a wire rack, standing the loaf on its base. Leave to cool.

Baker's tip
- This is not suitable for making as a larger loaf.

Sweet Potato Bread

This is a lovely moist bread with a slightly sweet flavour and beautiful, pale orange colour. Cut into chunky slices, it goes particularly well with spicy chilli and bean-based Caribbean dishes. A small amount of milk powder adds a creamy richness to the loaf.

- Put the sweet potatoes in a small pan and pour over just enough boiling water to cover. Bring to the boil, half cover the pan with a lid and simmer for 15 minutes or until tender. Drain, reserving the cooking liquid in a measuring jug. Make up to 175ml with cold water, if necessary, and leave until lukewarm.
- Meanwhile, mash the potatoes with the butter until very smooth.
- Lift the bread pan out of the bread machine and fit the kneading blade. Tip the warm mashed potato and the liquid into the pan. Add about half the flour, then the skimmed milk powder, then the rest of the flour.
- Put the salt and sugar in separate corners of the pan. Make a small hollow in the middle of the flour and add the yeast.
- Fit the pan into the bread machine, shut the lid and set to the basic white setting with a medium crust. Press start.
- Just before the loaf begins to bake, brush the top with milk.
- After baking, lift the pan out of the machine using oven gloves. Carefully shake out the loaf to remove it from the pan, then transfer to a wire rack, standing the loaf on its base. Leave to cool.

Baker's tips
- Make sure that the liquid and mashed sweet potato mixture are lukewarm, not hot, when you add the other ingredients.
- This is not suitable for making as a larger loaf.

Ingredients:
175g sweet potatoes, peeled and cut into small chunks
15g butter
400g strong white bread flour
2 tbsp skimmed milk powder
1 tsp salt
1 tsp golden caster sugar
1¼ tsp fast-action dried yeast
Milk, to brush

Quantities for a small (450g) loaf
100g sweet potatoes
10g butter
240g strong white bread flour
4 tsp skimmed milk powder
¾ tsp salt
¾ tsp golden caster sugar
¾ tsp fast-action dried yeast

Chilli Pepper Loaf

Ingredients:
300ml water
2 tbsp olive oil
500g strong white bread
   flour
2 fresh red chillies, halved,
   deseeded and finely
   chopped
2 tsp mild paprika
1¼ tsp salt
2 tsp caster sugar
1 tsp fast-action dried yeast

*Quantities for a large
   (900g) loaf*
360ml water
2½ tbsp olive oil
600g strong white bread
   flour
2 large fresh red chillies
2½ tsp mild paprika
1½ tsp salt
1 tbsp caster sugar
1¼ tsp fast-action dried
   yeast

*Quantities for a small
   (450g) loaf*
180ml water
1¼ tbsp olive oil
300g strong white bread
   flour
1 large fresh red chilli
1¼ tsp mild paprika
¾ tsp salt
1½ tsp caster sugar
¾ tsp fast-action dried yeast

This loaf is speckled with finely chopped red chillies added at the start of mixing so that their flavour can disperse throughout the loaf. If you want to tone down the heat, just use one chilli or choose a milder variety. Paprika adds a smoky subtleness to the flavour and colour.

- Lift the bread pan out of the bread machine and fit the kneading blade. Pour the water into the pan, then add the oil, followed by about half of the flour. Sprinkle the chopped red chillies and paprika over, then add the rest of the flour.
- Put the salt and sugar in separate corners of the pan, then make a shallow dip in the middle of the flour and add the yeast.
- Fit the pan into the bread machine, shut the lid and set to the basic white setting with a crust of your choice. Press start.
- After baking, lift the pan out of the machine using oven gloves. Carefully shake out the loaf to remove it from the pan, then transfer to a wire rack, standing the loaf on its base. Leave to cool.

Sun-dried Tomato and Olive Bread

This loaf has all the lovely sunny flavours of the Mediterranean: sun-dried tomatoes, olives and fragrant herbs, all added at the beginning of mixing. It's the perfect accompaniment to dishes such as French onion soup, minestrone, pâté, bolognaise and creamy pasta.

- Lift the bread pan out of the bread machine and fit the kneading blade. Pour the water into the pan, then add the oil, followed by about half of the flour. Sprinkle the chopped tomatoes, olives and herbs over, then add the rest of the flour.
- Put the salt and honey in separate corners of the pan, then make a shallow dip in the middle of the flour and add the yeast.
- Fit the pan into the bread machine, shut the lid and set to the basic white setting with a crust of your choice. Press start.
- After baking, lift the pan out of the machine using oven gloves. Carefully shake out the loaf to remove it from the pan, then transfer to a wire rack, standing the loaf on its base. Leave to cool.

Baker's tip
- Use other dried Mediterranean herbs if you prefer or buy ready-mixed dried Mediterranean herbs. You could also use fresh herbs such as chopped rosemary or even lavender flowers.

Ingredients:
300ml water
2 tbsp olive oil
500g strong white bread flour
50g sun-dried tomatoes in oil, drained and roughly chopped
50g pitted black olives in oil, drained and roughly chopped
1 tsp dried oregano
1 tsp dried thyme
1 tsp salt
1 tbsp clear honey
1 tsp fast-action dried yeast

Quantities for a large (1kg) loaf
360ml water
2½ tbsp olive oil
600g strong white bread flour
60g sun-dried tomatoes
60g pitted black olives
1¼ tsp dried oregano
1¼ tsp dried thyme
1¼ tsp salt
4 tsp clear honey
1¼ tsp fast-action dried yeast

Quantities for a small (500g) loaf
180ml water
1¼ tbsp olive oil
300g strong white bread flour
30g sun-dried tomatoes
30g black olives
¾ tsp dried oregano
¾ tsp dried thyme
¾ tsp salt
1½ tsp clear honey
¾ tsp fast-action dried yeast

Garlic Mushroom Bread

Ingredients:

50g dried porcini mushrooms
350ml boiling water
25g butter
1 garlic clove, peeled and
   crushed
75g strong wholemeal or
   brown bread flour
25g medium oatmeal plus
   extra for sprinkling
400g very strong white
   bread flour
1½ tsp salt
1 tbsp soft light brown sugar
1¼ tsp fast-action dried
   yeast

*Quantities for a large
   (900g) loaf*
50g dried porcini mushrooms
420ml boiling water
30g butter
1 large garlic clove
90g strong wholemeal or
   brown bread flour
30g medium oatmeal
480g strong white bread
   flour
1½ tsp salt
4 tsp soft light brown sugar
1¼ tsp fast-action dried
   yeast

While fresh mushrooms don't work well in machine-made bread, dried mushrooms are fantastic and add a deep, almost earthy taste. The hint of garlic allows the flavour of the mushrooms to shine; don't add more than one clove, as too much will inhibit the yeast.

- Put the dried mushrooms in a heatproof bowl and pour over the boiling water. Leave until the water is lukewarm and the mushrooms are soft. Drain the mushrooms, reserving the soaking liquid, then make up the liquid to 350ml with cold water. Finely chop the mushrooms.
- Lift the bread pan out of the bread machine and fit the kneading blade. Pour the water into the pan, then add the butter and garlic. Add the wholemeal flour and oatmeal, then sprinkle over the mushrooms. Add the white flour.
- Put the salt and sugar in separate corners of the pan, then make a shallow dip in the middle of the flour and add the yeast.
- Fit the pan into the bread machine, shut the lid and set to the basic white setting with a crust of your choice. Press start.
- After baking, lift the pan out of the machine using oven gloves. Carefully shake out the loaf to remove it from the pan, then transfer to a wire rack, standing the loaf on its base. Leave to cool.

Baker's tip
- Try using other dried mushrooms for a change. Larger supermarkets usually stock a wide range, including Portobello and shiitake and bags of mixed gourmet mushrooms for those who like them all.

Quantities for a small (450g) loaf

25g dried porcini mushrooms
210ml boiling water
15g butter
½ large garlic clove
45g strong wholemeal or brown bread
   flour

15g medium oatmeal
240g strong white bread flour
¾ tsp salt
2 tsp soft light brown sugar
¾ tsp fast-action dried yeast

Dill and Lemon Loaf

Subtly flavoured with fresh dill and fragrant lemon zest, this loaf is made with half wholemeal flour for its nutty taste and half white flour for a lighter texture. It's perfect for smoked salmon or cucumber sandwiches for a posh afternoon tea.

- Lift the bread pan out of the bread machine and fit the kneading blade. Pour in the water, then add the butter, followed by the wholemeal flour. Sprinkle over the dill and lemon zest and a generous seasoning of freshly ground black pepper. Add the white flour.
- Put the salt and sugar in separate corners of the pan. Then make a shallow dip in the middle of the flour and add the yeast.
- Fit the pan into the bread machine, shut the lid and set to the basic white setting with a crust of your choice. Press start.
- After baking, lift the pan out of the machine using oven gloves. Carefully shake out the loaf to remove it from the pan, then transfer to a wire rack, standing the loaf on its base. Leave to cool.

Ingredients:
325ml water
25g butter
250g strong wholemeal
   bread flour
3 tbsp chopped fresh dill
Finely grated zest of 1
   lemon
Freshly ground black
   pepper
250g strong white bread
   flour
1½ tsp salt
1 tbsp caster sugar
1¼ tsp fast-action dried
   yeast

Quantities for a large (900g) loaf
390ml water
30g butter
300g strong wholemeal bread flour
3½ tbsp chopped fresh dill
Finely grated zest of 1 lemon
Freshly ground black pepper
300g strong white bread flour
1¾ tsp salt
4 tsp caster sugar
1½ tsp fast-action dried yeast

Quantities for a small (450g) loaf
195ml water
15g butter
150g strong wholemeal bread flour
1½ tbsp chopped fresh dill
Finely grated zest of ½ lemon
Freshly ground black pepper
150g strong white bread flour
¾ tsp salt
2 tsp caster sugar
¾ tsp fast-action dried yeast

Carrot and Coriander Bread

Ingredients:
100ml hot (not boiling) water
150ml carrot juice
2 tbsp sunflower oil
1 tbsp clear honey
250g country grain, Granary or Malthouse flour
100g coarsely grated carrot
3 tbsp chopped fresh coriander
250g strong white bread flour
1¼ tsp salt
1 tsp fast-action dried yeast

A richly coloured, moist bread that's a great way to help you get your 5-a-day, carrots are naturally sweet and baking really develops their flavour. This is especially good with spicy dishes and is lovely served slightly warm with lentil-based soups and dips such as hummus.

- Lift the bread pan out of the bread machine and fit the kneading blade. Pour in the water and carrot juice, then add the oil and honey, followed by the country grain, Granary or Malthouse flour. Add the grated carrot and coriander and then the white bread flour.
- Put the salt and yeast in separate corners of the pan.
- Fit the pan into the bread machine, shut the lid and set to the wholewheat setting with a light crust. Press start.
- After baking, lift the pan out of the machine using oven gloves. Carefully shake out the loaf to remove it from the pan, then transfer to a wire rack, standing the loaf on its base. Leave to cool.

Baker's tip
- Check that the dough is a good consistency towards the end of mixing, and add a little more water or flour if necessary.

Quantities for a large (900g) loaf
120ml hot water
180ml carrot juice
2½ tbsp sunflower oil
4 tsp clear honey
300g country grain, Granary or Malthouse flour
120g coarsely grated carrot
3 tbsp chopped fresh coriander
300g strong white bread flour
1½ tsp salt
1¼ tsp fast-action dried yeast

Quantities for a small (450g) loaf
60ml hot water
90ml carrot juice
1¼ tbsp sunflower oil
2 tsp clear honey
150g country grain, Granary or Malthouse flour
60g coarsely grated carrot
1½ tbsp chopped fresh coriander
150g strong white bread flour
¾ tsp salt
¾ tsp fast-action dried yeast

Italian Blue Cheese Bread

An Italian duo of piquant Gorgonzola and robust Parmesan add a delicious flavour to this loaf. It's fantastic with Italian deli meats, such as salami, and sliced ripe plum tomatoes, or diced and sautéed in a little hot olive oil to serve as croûtons with soups such as minestrone.

- Lift the bread pan out of the bread machine and fit the kneading blade. Pour in the water, then add the olive oil, followed by the brown flour. Crumble over the Gorgonzola and add the Parmesan and oregano. Top with the white flour.
- Put the salt and sugar in separate corners of the pan. Then make a shallow dip in the middle of the flour and add the yeast.
- Fit the pan into the bread machine, shut the lid and set to the basic white setting with a crust of your choice. Press start.
- After baking, lift the pan out of the machine using oven gloves. Carefully shake out the loaf to remove it from the pan, then transfer to a wire rack, standing the loaf on its base. Leave to cool.

Ingredients:
325ml water
1 tbsp olive oil
250g strong brown bread
    flour
75g Gorgonzola cheese,
    crumbled
50g freshly grated
    Parmesan
1 tsp dried oregano
250g strong white bread
    flour
1 tsp salt
2 tsp caster sugar
1 tsp fast-action dried
    yeast

Quantities for a large (900g) loaf
390ml water
4 tsp olive oil
300g strong brown bread flour
90g Gorgonzola
60g Parmesan
1¼ tsp dried oregano
300g strong white bread flour
1¼ tsp salt
2 tsp caster sugar
1¼ tsp fast-action dried yeast

Quantities for a small (450g) loaf
195ml water
2 tsp olive oil
150g strong brown bread flour
45g Gorgonzola
30g Parmesan
¾ tsp dried oregano
150g strong white bread flour
¾ tsp salt
1 tsp caster sugar
¾ tsp fast-action dried yeast

Beetroot Bread

This unusual bread cooks to a vibrant pink, with a slightly earthy, sweet flavour. It is superb for sandwiches with smoked ham or mild cheeses with pickles. You'll achieve an even richer colour and flavour by substituting 75ml of beetroot juice for the same amount of water.

Ingredients:
200ml water
150g cooked and peeled beetroot in natural juices, drained and coarsely grated
1 tbsp sunflower oil
1 tsp balsamic vinegar
425g strong white bread flour
1¼ tsp salt
2 tsp soft light brown sugar
1¼ tsp fast-action dried yeast

Quantities for a large (900g) loaf
240ml water
180g cooked beetroot
1½ tbsp sunflower oil
1¼ tsp balsamic vinegar
510g strong white bread flour
1½ tsp salt
1 tbsp soft light brown sugar
1½ tsp fast-action dried yeast

Quantities for a small (450g) loaf
120ml water
90g cooked beetroot
2 tsp sunflower oil
¾ tsp balsamic vinegar
255g strong white bread flour
¾ tsp salt
1½ tsp soft light brown sugar
¾ tsp fast-action dried yeast

- Lift the bread pan out of the bread machine and fit the kneading blade. Pour in the water, then add the beetroot, oil and vinegar, followed by the flour.
- Put the salt and sugar in separate corners of the pan. Then make a shallow dip in the middle of the flour and add the yeast.
- Fit the pan into the bread machine, shut the lid and set to the basic white setting with a light or medium crust. Press start.
- After baking, lift the pan out of the machine using oven gloves. Carefully shake out the loaf to remove it from the pan, then transfer to a wire rack, standing the loaf on its base. Leave to cool.

Baker's tips
- Make sure you use fresh beetroot in natural juices (or vacuum packed) and not those pickled in vinegar. Drain and gently pat dry on kitchen paper before grating. Beetroot can stain your hands, so wear clean rubber or plastic gloves if you want to prevent this.
- Check the dough towards the end of mixing and add a tablespoon more water or flour, if necessary; this will depend on how moist the beetroot is.

Hot Potato and Horseradish Bread

The addition of freshly cooked mashed potato makes a moist and light-textured loaf, perfect with hot soups and casseroles on cold wintry days or toasted and topped with browned and bubbling sliced or grated cheese. The horseradish gives extra 'bite' so use less if you prefer.

Ingredients:
200g potatoes, peeled and cut into chunks
1 bay leaf
Boiling water
25g butter
1¼ tsp salt
Freshly ground black pepper
1 tbsp hot horseradish sauce
425g strong white bread flour
2 tsp caster sugar
1¼ tsp fast-action dried yeast

- Put the potatoes in a pan with the bay leaf and barely cover with boiling water. Bring to the boil, reduce the heat, half cover the pan with a lid and simmer for 15 minutes or until just tender. Drain, reserving the cooking liquid. Discard the bay leaf.
- Return the potatoes to the pan, add the butter, salt and pepper. Mash until very smooth, then stir in the horseradish.
- Lift the bread pan out of the bread machine and fit the kneading blade. Measure 150ml of the cooking liquid in a jug, topping up with cold water if necessary. When both the potato and liquid have cooled to lukewarm, put them in the bread pan. Add the flour.
- Put the sugar and yeast in separate corners of the pan.
- Fit the pan into the bread machine, shut the lid and set to the basic white setting with a crust of your choice. Press start.
- After baking, lift the pan out of the machine using oven gloves. Carefully shake out the loaf to remove it from the pan, then transfer to a wire rack, standing the loaf on its base. Leave to cool.

Quantities for a large (900g) loaf
240g potatoes
1 bay leaf
30g butter
1½ tsp salt
Freshly ground black pepper
4 tsp hot horseradish sauce
510g strong white bread flour
1 tbsp caster sugar
1½ tsp fast-action dried yeast

Quantities for a small (450g) loaf
120g potatoes
1 bay leaf
15g butter
¾ tsp salt
Freshly ground black pepper
2 tsp hot horseradish sauce
255g strong white bread flour
1½ tsp caster sugar
¾ tsp fast-action dried yeast

Celery and Walnut Loaf

Ingredients:
75g walnut pieces, roughly chopped
25g butter
2 celery sticks, finely chopped
300ml water
75g buckwheat flour
400g strong white bread flour
1 tsp celery salt or salt
1 tbsp soft light brown sugar
1 tsp fast-action dried yeast

This loaf contains a little buckwheat flour, which adds to the nutty taste and texture. Although it takes a bit longer to prepare, it is worth toasting the walnuts and sautéing the celery to enhance their flavour. Using the wholewheat cycle produces a lighter loaf.

- Cook the walnut pieces in a non-stick frying pan over a low heat for 3–4 minutes, stirring or shaking the pan frequently until they have a nutty aroma. Tip onto a plate and leave to cool.
- Melt the butter in the pan. Add the celery and gently cook for 4–5 minutes, stirring occasionally, until just tender.
- Lift the bread pan out of the bread machine and fit the kneading blade. Tip in the cooked celery. Pour in the water, then add the flours. Put the salt and sugar in separate corners of the pan. Then make a shallow dip in the middle of the flour and add the yeast.
- Put the walnuts in the automatic dispenser if your machine has one.
- Fit the pan into the bread machine, shut the lid and set to the wholewheat setting with a crust of your choice. Press start.
- If your machine doesn't have an automatic dispenser, add the walnuts when the machine bleeps, or halfway through the kneading time.
- After baking, lift the pan out of the machine using oven gloves. Carefully shake out the loaf to remove it from the pan, then transfer to a wire rack, standing the loaf on its base. Leave to cool.

Quantities for a large (900g) loaf
90g walnut pieces
30g butter
2 large celery sticks, finely chopped
360ml water
90g buckwheat flour
480g strong white bread flour
1¼ tsp celery salt or salt
4 tsp soft light brown
1¼ tsp fast-action dried yeast

Quantities for a small (450g) loaf
45g walnut pieces
15g butter
1 large celery stick, finely chopped
180ml water
45g buckwheat flour
240g strong white bread flour
¾ tsp celery salt or salt
2 tsp soft light brown sugar
¾ tsp fast-action dried yeast

Poppy Seed Loaf

This light and airy loaf is speckled with poppy seeds, which add a lovely texture and subtle flavour. Popular in Eastern Europe, this bread goes particularly well with creamy soups or more hearty vegetable versions. Toasting the poppy seeds enhances their nutty flavour.

- Put 4 tbsp of the poppy seeds in a small frying pan and cook over a low heat for 2–3 minutes, stirring or shaking the pan occasionally, until lightly toasted. Remove from the heat.
- Lift the bread pan out of the bread machine and fit the kneading blade. Pour in the water, then add the butter followed by about half of the flour. Sprinkle over the milk powder, followed by the rest of the flour.
- Put the salt and sugar in separate corners of the pan, then make a shallow dip in the middle and add the yeast.
- Put the poppy seeds in the automatic dispenser if your machine has one.
- Fit the pan into the bread machine, shut the lid and set to the basic white setting with a light or medium crust. Press start.
- If your machine doesn't have an automatic dispenser, add the poppy seeds when the machine bleeps or halfway through the kneading time.
- Just before baking, brush the top of the loaf with water or milk and sprinkle with the remaining 1 tbsp poppy seeds.
- After baking, lift the pan out of the machine using oven gloves. Carefully shake out the loaf to remove it from the pan, then transfer to a wire rack, standing the loaf on its base. Leave to cool.

Ingredients:
5 tbsp poppy seeds
325ml water
25g butter
500g strong white bread flour
2 tbsp skimmed milk powder
1 tsp salt
1 tbsp caster sugar
1 tsp fast-action dried yeast

Quantities for a large (900g) loaf
6 tbsp poppy seeds
390ml water
30g butter
600g strong white bread flour
2 tbsp skimmed milk powder
1¼ tsp salt
4 tsp caster sugar
1¼ tsp fast-action dried yeast

Quantities for a small (450g) loaf
3 tbsp poppy seeds
195ml water
15g butter
300g strong white bread flour
1 tbsp skimmed milk powder
¾ tsp salt
2 tsp caster sugar
¾ tsp fast-action dried yeast

Butternut Squash Bread

Ingredients:
1 butternut squash,
    weighing 600–650g
2 tbsp water
1 tbsp sunflower oil
1 tbsp golden caster sugar
1¼ tsp salt
425g strong white bread
    flour
1 tsp fast-action dried yeast

*Quantities for a large
    (900g) loaf*
725g butternut squash
    (480g diced flesh)
2 tbsp water
4 tsp sunflower oil
1½ tsp salt
4 tsp golden caster sugar
500g strong white bread
    flour
1¼ tsp fast action dried
    yeast

*Quantities for a small
    (450g) loaf*
½ x 725g butternut squash
    (240g diced flesh)
1 tbsp water
2 tsp sunflower oil
¾ tsp salt
2 tsp golden caster sugar
250g strong white bread
    flour
¾ tsp fast action dried yeast

The addition of butternut squash purée makes a wonderfully fine, soft bread with a fantastic golden colour, excellent for toasting and an easy way to include more veg in your diet. Use any winter squash – it's great for using up hollowed out pumpkin flesh at Hallowe'en.

- Halve and peel the butternut squash, then scoop out the fibrous core and seeds. Dice the flesh into small cubes; you should have about 400g. Put the butternut squash in a bowl and sprinkle over the water. Tightly cover with clingfilm and microwave for 4–5 minutes or until tender. Leave to cool for a few minutes.
- Put in a food processor with the oil, salt and sugar and blend until smooth.
- Lift the bread pan out of the bread machine and fit the kneading blade. Add the purée followed by the flour. Make a shallow dip in the middle and add the yeast.
- Fit the pan into the bread machine, shut the lid and set to the basic white setting with a light or medium crust. Press start.
- After baking, lift the pan out of the machine using oven gloves. Carefully shake out the loaf to remove it from the pan, then transfer to a wire rack, standing the loaf on its base. Leave to cool.

Baker's tips
- For extra flavour and texture, add 2–3 tbsp pumpkin seeds either in the automatic dispenser, if you have one, or when your machine bleeps or halfway through the kneading time.
- If you don't have a microwave, put the diced squash in a pan, just cover with boiling water, cover and simmer for about 15 minutes until tender, then drain well, reserving 2 tbsp of the water and adding it when you purée the squash.

Mediterranean Vegetable Bread

Packets of dried vegetables are readily available in supermarkets and make great storecupboard standbys. They minimise preparation time and their flavour is more intense than fresh vegetables. Try serving this with deli meats such as salami and sliced cheeses.

- Put the vegetables in a heatproof bowl and pour over enough boiling water to cover them. Leave for 15 minutes or until the vegetables have softened. Drain well, reserving the soaking liquid. Chop the vegetables into small pieces and make up the liquid to 300ml with cold water.
- Lift the bread pan out of the bread machine and fit the kneading blade. Pour the water into the pan. Add the vegetables, oil and herbs, followed by the flour.
- Put the salt and sugar in separate corners of the pan, then make a shallow dip in the middle and add the yeast.
- Fit the pan into the bread machine, shut the lid and set to the French bread setting with a crust of your choice. Press start.
- After baking, lift the pan out of the machine using oven gloves. Carefully shake out the loaf to remove it from the pan, then transfer to a wire rack, standing the loaf on its base. Leave to cool.

Baker's tips
- You can often buy mixed packets of dried mixed vegetables containing aubergines, courgettes and tomatoes. Dried onions also work well in this recipe and are the least expensive option, in which case you don't need to chop them.
- If you want the vegetables to retain their shape and be less blended with the dough, add them when the machine bleeps or halfway through the kneading time. Do not place in the automatic dispenser, as they may stick.

Ingredients:
40g dried vegetables
Boiling water, for soaking
2 tsp olive oil
1 tsp dried Mediterranean herbs or mixed herbs
450g Type 55 French flour
1 tsp celery salt or ordinary salt
2 tsp caster sugar
1 tsp fast-action dried yeast

Quantities for a large (900g) loaf
50g dried vegetables
Boiling water, for soaking (make up to 360ml with cold water)
2½ tsp olive oil
1¼ tsp dried herbs
540g Type 55 French flour
1¼ tsp salt
1 tbsp caster sugar
1¼ tsp fast-action dried yeast

Quantities for a small (450g) loaf
25g dried vegetables
Boiling water, for soaking (make up to 180ml with cold water)
1¼ tsp olive oil
¾ tsp dried herbs
270g Type 55 French flour
¾ tsp salt
1½ tsp caster sugar
¾ tsp fast-action dried yeast

Indian Spiced Bread

Ingredients:
300ml lukewarm water
2 tsp cumin seeds
2 tbsp groundnut oil
2 tbsp curry paste
400g can chickpeas, drained
    and rinsed
450g strong white bread
    flour
1½ tsp salt
1 tbsp golden caster sugar
1½ tsp fast-action dried
    yeast

*Quantities for a small
    (450g) loaf*
150ml lukewarm water
1 tsp cumin seeds
1 tbsp groundnut oil
1 tbsp curry paste
200g can chickpeas, drained
    and rinsed
225g strong white bread
    flour
¾ tsp salt
1½ tsp golden caster sugar
¾ tsp fast-action dried yeast

- Lift the bread pan out of the bread machine and fit the kneading blade. Pour the water into the pan.
- Lightly crush the cumin seeds; on a board with the back of a tablespoon is fine, if you don't have a pestle and mortar. Put in a bowl with the oil, curry paste and chickpeas and roughly mash together with a fork. Add to the pan, followed by the flour.
- Put the salt and sugar in separate corners of the pan, then make a shallow dip in the middle and add the yeast.
- Fit the pan into the bread machine, shut the lid and set to the basic white setting with a crust of your choice. Press start.
- After baking, lift the pan out of the machine using oven gloves. Carefully shake out the loaf to remove it from the pan, then transfer to a wire rack, standing the loaf on its base. Leave to cool.

Baker's tip
- Use your favourite curry paste for this bread. Korma makes a fragrant and mildly spiced loaf, or try a medium curry paste; Madras and Jalfrezi both work well.

Smoky Bacon and Maple Syrup Brioche

Bacon and maple syrup are a classic complementary combination, here flavouring a buttery brioche bread that is still very much a savoury loaf with the maple syrup providing just a hint of sweetness; it's fantastic for a substantial breakfast, topped with poached or fried eggs.

- Snip the bacon into small pieces using kitchen scissors. Dry-fry in a non-stick pan over a medium heat for 4–5 minutes or until lightly browned.
- Lift the bread pan out of the bread machine and fit the kneading blade. Add the bacon and any fat in the pan.
- Whisk the eggs together with a fork in a jug, then add enough milk to reach the 250ml mark. Add the maple syrup and stir together. Pour into the bread pan. Add the butter and the flour.
- Put the salt and yeast in separate corners of the pan.
- Fit the pan into the bread machine, shut the lid and set to the sweet bread or brioche setting with a light crust. Press start.
- After baking, lift the pan out of the machine using oven gloves. Carefully shake out the loaf to remove it from the pan, then transfer to a wire rack, standing the loaf on its base. Leave to cool.

Baker's tips
- Taste the bacon after dry-frying. If it is quite salty, reduce the amount of salt to ½ tsp.
- This is not suitable for making as a large loaf.

Ingredients:
4 rashers smoked streaky bacon, rind removed
2 medium eggs
About 150ml milk
3 tbsp maple syrup
75g butter, at room temperature
450g strong white bread flour
¾ tsp salt
1¼ tsp fast-action dried yeast

Quantities for a small (450g) loaf
3 rashers smoked streaky bacon, rind removed
2 small eggs (make up to 150ml with milk)
2 tbsp maple syrup
45g butter
275g strong white bread flour
½ tsp salt
¾ tsp fast-action dried yeast

Sweet Enriched Breads

Bread doesn't have to be savoury; fresh and dried fruit-flavoured loaves, nuts and chocolate are all featured. These are breads to serve as a special treat for breakfast or a lazy brunch, using the delay timer overnight, or for a coffee-break or tea-time treat instead of serving cakes and cookies. Many are blissfully simple to make, others take a little more time to prepare the ingredients, but all will tempt both your eye and your palate.

CHAPTER 7

Candied Fruit and Cardamom Loaf

Ingredients:
4 cardamom pods
150ml milk
150ml water
25g butter, softened
100g almond paste
   (marzipan), roughly
   chopped
500g strong white bread
   flour
75g candied fruit, finely
   chopped
50g toasted flaked almonds
1½ tsp salt
1 tbsp golden caster sugar
1½ tsp fast-action dried
   yeast

To serve
2 tsp icing sugar (optional),
   to dust

*Quantities for a small
   (450g) loaf*
2 cardamom pods
75ml milk
75ml water
15g butter
50g marzipan
250g strong white bread flour
35g candied fruit
25g toasted flaked almonds
¾ tsp salt
1½ tsp golden caster sugar
¾ tsp fast-action dried yeast
1 tsp icing sugar, to dust

This is a simplified version of Christmas stollen and gets its lovely flavour from a pairing of almond paste and toasted nuts. The almond paste blends into the dough during kneading, so choose yellow rather than white almond paste to give the loaf a stunning golden colour.

- Remove the cardamom seeds and discard the husks. Finely crush the seeds with a pestle and mortar or on a board with the back of a spoon.
- Lift the bread pan out of the bread machine and fit the kneading blade. Pour in the milk and water and add the butter and marzipan, followed by about half of the flour.
- Sprinkle over the crushed cardamom, the fruit and almonds, then top with the remaining flour.
- Put the salt and sugar in separate corners of the pan, then make a shallow dip in the middle of the flour and add the yeast.
- Fit the pan into the bread machine, shut the lid and set to the basic white setting with a light crust. Press start.
- After baking, lift the pan out of the machine using oven gloves. Carefully shake out the loaf to remove it from the pan, then transfer to a wire rack, standing the loaf on its base. Leave to cool.
- Dust the top with a little icing sugar just before serving, if liked.

Baker's tip
- Choose a mixture of candied fruit for this loaf, such as good-quality candied orange and lemon peel, cherries, pineapple and ginger.

Quick Oat and Apple Loaf

Although you need to pre-cook the apples for this loaf, it is then baked on the fast setting, so should be ready in a couple of hours. There's no need to wait for it to cool completely, either, as it's delicious served slightly warm and lightly spread with butter.

- Heat the butter in a non-stick frying pan until melted. Add the apples and stir to coat in the butter, then cover with a lid and cook over a low heat for 3–4 minutes. Uncover, sprinkle over the sugar and turn up the heat a little. Cook, stirring, until the apples just start to colour. Turn off the heat and leave for 2–3 minutes to cool a little.
- Lift the bread pan out of the bread machine and fit the kneading blade. Tip the warm apple mixture into the pan and pour over the apple juice and water. Add the oatmeal, cinnamon and flour.
- Put the salt and yeast in separate corners of the pan.
- Fit the pan into the bread machine, shut the lid and set to the rapid (about 2 hour) setting with a medium crust. Press start.
- After baking, lift the pan out of the machine using oven gloves. Carefully shake out the loaf to remove it from the pan, then transfer to a wire rack, standing the loaf on its base. Leave to cool.

Baker's tips
- Try making this with fresh pears and pear or orange juice, for a change, substituting ground ginger for the cinnamon.
- This is not suitable for making as a larger loaf.
- If you're not in a hurry, bake this on the sweet bread setting using just 1 tsp fast-action dried yeast.

Ingredients:
25g unsalted butter
2 eating apples, peeled, cored and cut into 1cm chunks
2 tbsp golden caster sugar
175ml apple juice
100ml water
50g medium oatmeal
2 tsp ground cinnamon
400g strong white bread flour
1 tsp salt
1¼ tsp fast-action dried yeast

Quantities for a small (450g) loaf
15g unsalted butter
1 large eating apple
2 tsp golden caster sugar
100ml apple juice
65ml water
30g medium oatmeal
1 tsp ground cinnamon
250g strong white bread flour
¾ tsp salt
¾ tsp fast-action dried yeast

Malted Fruit Bread

Ingredients:
3 tbsp malt extract
150ml hot water
150ml cold water
50g butter
150g strong brown bread
    flour
50g soft dark brown sugar
3 tbsp skimmed milk powder
350g strong white bread
    flour
1 tsp salt
1¼ tsp fast-action dried
    yeast
100g mixed dried fruit
1 tsp icing sugar

*Quantities for a small
   (500g) loaf*
90ml hot water
2 tbsp malt extract
90ml cold water
30g butter
90g strong brown bread
    flour
30g soft dark brown sugar
2 tbsp skimmed milk powder
210g strong white bread
    flour
½ tsp salt
¾ tsp fast action dried fruit
60g mixed dried fruit
¾ tsp icing sugar

Dark and sticky malt extract gives a fantastic depth of flavour and colour to this sweet barley bread. Lightly dotted with fruit, it has a slightly chewy texture but isn't overly sweet. Use a good quality 'luxury' dried fruit mix which is pre-soaked so the fruit is plump and juicy.

- Lift the bread pan out of the bread machine and fit the kneading blade. Stir the malt extract into the hot water until blended, then stir in the cold water. Pour into the bread pan. Add the butter and brown flour, top with the sugar and skimmed milk powder, then add the white flour.
- Put the salt and yeast in separate corners of the pan.
- Put the fruit in the automatic dispenser if you have one.
- Fit the pan into the bread machine, shut the lid and set to the sweet bread setting with a light crust. Press start.
- If you don't have an automatic dispenser, add the fruit when the machine bleeps or halfway through the kneading time.
- After baking, lift the pan out of the machine using oven gloves. Carefully shake out the loaf to remove it from the pan, then transfer to a wire rack, standing the loaf on its base. Leave to cool.
- Dust the top with icing sugar before serving.

Baker's tip
- This loaf is also good made with finely chopped dried dates instead of the mixed fruit.

Chocolate and Banana Bread

This makes a delicious breakfast bread or tea-time treat and for both children and sweet-toothed adults. It's an ideal way to use up over-ripe bananas languishing in the fruit bowl. The chocolate partially melts as the warm dough rises, giving a lovely marbled effect to the loaf.

- Lift the bread pan out of the bread machine and fit the kneading blade. Pour in the milk and add the butter. Mash the bananas until fairly smooth, then add to the bread pan followed by about half of the flour. Sprinkle over the chocolate chips then top with the remaining flour.
- Put the salt and sugar in separate corners of the pan, then make a shallow dip in the middle of the flour and add the yeast.
- Fit the pan into the bread machine, shut the lid and set to the basic white setting with a light crust. Press start.
- After baking, lift the pan out of the machine using oven gloves. Carefully shake out the loaf to remove it from the pan, then transfer to a wire rack, standing the loaf on its base. Leave to cool.
- Dust the top with a little icing sugar just before serving, if liked.

Baker's tips
- If you prefer a less melted chocolate marbled effect, add the chocolate chips when the machine beeps or halfway through kneading.
- This is not suitable for making as a larger loaf.

Ingredients:
275ml milk
25g butter, softened
2 small or 1 large ripe banana
450g strong white bread flour
75g plain chocolate chips
1¼ tsp salt
2 tsp golden caster sugar
1 tsp fast-action dried yeast
1 tsp icing sugar (optional)

Quantities for a small (500g) loaf
165ml milk
15g butter
1 medium ripe banana
270g strong white bread flour
45g plain chocolate chips
¾ tsp salt
1 tsp golden caster sugar
¾ tsp fast-action dried yeast

Rum and Raisin Bread

Ingredients:
100g seedless raisins
3 tbsp rum
Finely grated zest and juice
   of 1 orange
About 250ml water
25g butter
500g strong white bread
   flour
25g golden caster or dark
   muscovado sugar
1¼ tsp salt
1 tsp fast-action dried yeast

To glaze
75g golden icing sugar
3 tbsp rum

*Quantities for a small
   (475g) loaf*
60g seedless raisins
2 tbsp rum
Finely grated zest and juice
   of 1 small orange (make
   up to 180ml with cold
   water)
About 150ml water
300g strong white bread
   flour
15g golden caster or dark
   muscovado sugar
¾ tsp salt
¾ tsp fast-action dried yeast

To glaze
50g golden caster sugar
2 tbsp rum

Here, raisins are soaked in rum until plump and juicy, then added to a sweet bread dough flavoured with orange zest. Allow extra time to soak the raisins (or remember to do this the night before). The loaf is finished with an optional sticky rum glaze.

- Put the raisins in a small bowl and spoon over the rum. Stir, then cover with clingfilm and leave to soak for at least 2 hours and for up to 24 hours.
- Lift the bread pan out of the bread machine and fit the kneading blade. Put the orange zest and juice in a jug and make up to 300ml with cold water. Pour into the bread pan, then add butter and about half of the flour.
- Sprinkle over the sugar, then top with the remaining flour. Put the salt and yeast in separate corners of the pan.
- Fit the pan into the bread machine, shut the lid and set to the basic white setting with a light crust. Press start.
- When the machine bleeps or halfway through the kneading time, add the raisins and any unabsorbed rum.
- After baking, lift the pan out of the machine using oven gloves. Carefully shake out the loaf to remove it from the pan, then transfer to a wire rack, standing the loaf on its base. Leave to cool.
- Shortly before serving, sift the icing into a bowl and stir in the rum until smooth. Spoon the icing over the top of the loaf, letting it dribble down the sides. Leave to set.

Baker's tips
- You can either use white or dark rum for this recipe; use golden caster sugar if you choose white and dark muscovado for dark rum. If preferred, you could make a non-alcoholic raisin and orange loaf, by using orange juice instead of rum.
- This is not suitable for making as a larger loaf.

Dark Chocolate and Almond Panettone

This Italian-style bread has a rich mixture of dark chocolate, cocoa, butter and egg, so it needs a little extra yeast and warm liquid to ensure it rises sufficiently. It's delicious spread with mascarpone or ricotta cheese and drizzled with a little honey.

- Pour about a third of the milk into a small pan. Add the butter and heat gently until the butter has melted. Stir in the rest of the milk, the vanilla and egg.
- Lift the bread pan out of the bread machine and fit the kneading blade. Add the milk and butter mixture, followed by the chocolate and about half the flour.
- Add the cocoa powder and sugar, then top with the rest of the flour.
- Put the salt and yeast in separate corners of the pan.
- Put the almonds in the automatic dispenser if you have one.
- Fit the pan into the bread machine, shut the lid and set to the sweet bread setting with a light crust. Press start.
- If you don't have an automatic dispenser, add the flaked almonds when the machine bleeps or halfway through the kneading time.
- After baking, lift the pan out of the machine using oven gloves. Carefully shake out the loaf to remove it from the pan, then transfer to a wire rack, standing the loaf on its base. Leave to cool.

Baker's tips
- For a fruit panettone, leave out the chocolate chips and flaked almonds and add 100g mixed dried fruit in the automatic dispenser or part-way through the kneading time. Replace the cocoa powder with the same amount of strong white bread flour and the soft light brown sugar with caster sugar.
- This is not suitable for making as a larger loaf.

Ingredients:
200ml milk
40g butter
2 tsp vanilla extract
1 medium egg, lightly beaten
100g plain chocolate chips or plain chocolate, finely chopped
375g strong white bread flour
25g cocoa powder
50g soft light brown sugar
¼ tsp salt
1¼ tsp fast-action dried yeast
50g toasted flaked almonds

Quantities for a small (450g) loaf
120ml milk
25g butter
1 tsp vanilla extract
1 small egg, lightly beaten
60g plain chocolate
225g strong white bread flour
15g cocoa powder
30g soft light brown sugar
Pinch of salt
¾ tsp fast-action dried yeast
30g toasted flaked almonds

Creamy Coconut, Pineapple and Papaya Loaf

Ingredients:
100g creamed coconut, chopped
150ml boiling water
150ml milk
20g butter
450g strong white bread flour
50g caster sugar
½ tsp salt
1¼ tsp fast-action dried yeast
100g ready-to-eat dried pineapple and papaya (or tropical fruit mix), chopped if necessary
Icing sugar, to dust

Quantities for a small (450g) loaf
90ml boiling water
60g creamed coconut, chopped
90ml milk
270g strong white bread flour
30g caster sugar
¾ tsp salt
¾ tsp fast-action dried yeast
60g ready-to-eat dried pineapple and papaya

This sweet bread contains creamed coconut, which gives a lovely moist and almost cake-like texture. It's dotted with chunks of colourful, ready-to-eat dried pineapple and papaya, but you can use a mixture of dried tropical fruits, if you prefer.

- Add the creamed coconut to the boiling water and stir until dissolved (it doesn't matter if it doesn't dissolve completely).
- Lift the bread pan out of the bread machine and fit the kneading blade. Pour in the coconut mixture. Add the milk and butter. Add about half of the flour, top with the sugar, then the rest of the flour.
- Put the salt and yeast in separate corners of the pan.
- Put the fruit in the automatic dispenser if you have one.
- Fit the pan into the bread machine, shut the lid and set to the sweet bread setting with a light crust. Press start.
- If you don't have an automatic dispenser, add the fruit when the machine bleeps or halfway through the kneading time.
- After baking, lift the pan out of the machine using oven gloves. Carefully shake out the loaf to remove it from the pan, then transfer to a wire rack, standing the loaf on its base. Leave to cool.
- Dust the top with icing sugar before serving.

Baker's tip
- This is not suitable for making as a larger loaf.

Cider and Apple Bread

Cider gives this loaf a fantastic flavour and aroma, but don't worry, all the alcohol evaporates as it bakes. Dried apples are the obvious choice of fruit to add to the loaf, but dried pears (and perry – pear cider) or dried peaches would also work well.

- Lift the bread pan out of the bread machine and fit the kneading blade. Pour in the cider and add the chopped apples. Leave to soak for 15 minutes.
- Add the butter, flour and cinnamon.
- Put the sugar and salt in separate corners of the pan, then make a hollow in the middle and add the yeast.
- Fit the pan into the bread machine, shut the lid and set to the sweet bread setting with a light crust. Press start.
- After baking, lift the pan out of the machine using oven gloves. Carefully shake out the loaf to remove it from the pan, then transfer to a wire rack, standing the loaf on its base. Leave to cool.

Baker's tips
- There are many different ciders to choose from, including pear and soft berry varieties. Choose a sweet or medium one with a robust flavour, though, as delicate flavours will be overpowered in the bread.
- This is not suitable for making as a larger loaf.

Ingredients:
350ml sweet cider
75g dried apples, chopped
25g butter
500g strong white bread
    flour
2 tsp ground cinnamon
2 tbsp golden caster sugar
½ tsp salt
1 tsp fast-action dried
    yeast

*Quantities for a small
    (475g) loaf*
200ml sweet cider
50g dried apples, chopped
15g butter
300g strong white bread
    flour
1 tsp ground cinnamon
4 tsp golden caster sugar
Large pinch of salt
¾ tsp fast-action dried
    yeast

Makes a 850g loaf

Buttery Brioche Bread

Ingredients:
2 medium eggs
About 175ml milk
100g butter, at room
    temperature
450g strong white bread
    flour
50g caster sugar
1 tsp salt
1¼ tsp fast-action dried
    yeast

*Quantities for a small
    (450g) loaf*
2 small eggs (make up to
    165ml with milk)
60g butter
275g strong white bread
    flour
30g caster sugar
¾ tsp salt
¾ tsp fast-action dried yeast

Enriched with milk, butter and eggs, this French bread has a wonderful soft texture and is superb when lightly toasted. Traditionally it is made in individual moulds and has a fluted bottom and topknot, but making it as a loaf in a bread machine is far less time-consuming.

- Lift the bread pan out of the bread machine and fit the kneading blade. Whisk the eggs together with a fork in a jug, then add enough milk to reach the 275ml mark. Pour into the bread pan. Add the butter and about half of the flour. Add the sugar, then the rest of the flour.
- Put the salt and yeast in separate corners of the pan.
- Fit the pan into the bread machine, shut the lid and set to the sweet bread setting with a light crust. Press start.
- After baking, lift the pan out of the machine using oven gloves. Carefully shake out the loaf to remove it from the pan, then transfer to a wire rack, standing the loaf on its base. Leave to cool.

Baker's tip
- This is not suitable for making as a larger loaf.

Toasted Hazelnut and Chocolate Brioche

Hazelnuts and chocolate are a great combination in this buttery brioche. As it's not overly sweet it makes a great weekend brunch toast. A dusting of icing sugar adds an attractive finish, but do this just before serving or it will soak in and make the top sticky.

- Put the hazelnuts in a small non-stick frying pan and gently toast over a low heat for 2–4 minutes, stirring or shaking the pan frequently until they smell aromatic and are just beginning to colour. Leave to cool for a few minutes.
- Meanwhile, lift the bread pan out of the bread machine and fit the kneading blade. Whisk the eggs together with a fork in a jug, then add enough milk to reach the 275ml mark. Pour into the bread pan. Add the butter and about half of the flour. Add cocoa and sugar, then the rest of the flour.
- Put the salt and yeast in separate corners of the pan.
- Put the nuts in the automatic dispenser if your machine has one.
- Fit the pan into the bread machine, shut the lid and set to the sweet bread setting with a light crust. Press start.
- If you don't have an automatic dispenser, add the nuts when the machine bleeps, or halfway through the kneading time.
- After baking, lift the pan out of the machine using oven gloves. Carefully shake out the loaf to remove it from the pan, then transfer to a wire rack, standing the loaf on its base. Leave to cool.

Baker's tip
- This is not suitable for making as a larger loaf.

Ingredients:
100g skinned hazelnuts, roughly chopped
2 medium eggs
About 175ml milk
100g butter, at room temperature
425g strong white bread flour
25g cocoa powder
50g soft light brown sugar
1 tsp salt
1¼ tsp fast-action dried yeast

Quantities for a small (500g) loaf
60g skinned hazelnuts
2 small eggs (make up to 165ml with milk)
60g butter
255g strong white bread flour
15g cocoa powder
30g soft light brown sugar
¾ tsp salt
¾ tsp fast-action dried yeast

Sweet Saffron and Honey Bread

Saffron is one of the most expensive spices you can buy, but you'll only need a pinch of this spice to add an exotic fragrance and stunning golden colour. Choose a mild-flavoured honey and a good-quality vanilla extract rather than 'essence' to subtly enhance the final flavour.

- Pour the milk into a small saucepan. Add the saffron and heat gently until steaming hot. Turn off the heat and leave for 20 minutes or until the milk is barely warm. Stir in the honey and vanilla extract.
- Lift the bread pan out of the bread machine and fit the kneading blade. Pour in the saffron mixture and add the butter, then the flour.
- Put the salt and yeast in separate corners of the pan.
- Fit the pan into the bread machine, shut the lid and set to the sweet bread setting with a light crust. Press start.
- After baking, lift the pan out of the machine using oven gloves. Carefully shake out the loaf to remove it from the pan, then transfer to a wire rack, standing the loaf on its base. Leave to cool.

Ingredients:
300ml milk
Large pinch of saffron
   strands
3 tbsp clear honey
1 tsp vanilla extract
30g butter
500g strong white bread
   flour
1 tsp salt
1 tsp fast-action dried yeast

*Quantities for a large
   (900g) loaf*
360ml milk
Large pinch of saffron
   strands
3½ tbsp clear honey
1¼ tsp vanilla extract
40g butter
600g strong white bread
   flour
1¼ tsp salt
1¼ tsp fast-action dried
   yeast

*Quantities for a small
   (450g) loaf*
180ml milk
Pinch of saffron strands
2 tbsp clear honey
¾ tsp vanilla extract
20g butter
300g strong white bread
   flour
¾ tsp salt
¾ tsp fast-action dried yeast

Fig and Rosemary Bread

This loaf has a taste and aroma reminiscent of the Mediterranean and is based on the sweet breads you can buy in Greek bakeries, enriched with strong-scented dark honey and dark green olive oil. Rosemary is a strong-flavoured herb, so don't be tempted to add extra.

- Lift the bread pan out of the bread machine and fit the kneading blade. Stir the honey into the water, then pour into the bread pan. Add the oil. Add half the spelt flour, then sprinkle over the rosemary before adding the rest of the flour.
- Put the yeast and salt in separate corners of the pan.
- Put the chopped figs in the automatic dispenser if your machine has one.
- Fit the pan into the bread machine, shut the lid and set to the sweet bread setting with a light crust. Press start.
- If your machine doesn't have an automatic dispenser, add the figs when the machine bleeps or halfway through the kneading time.
- After baking, lift the pan out of the machine using oven gloves. Carefully shake out the loaf to remove it from the pan, then transfer to a wire rack, standing the loaf on its base. Leave to cool.

Ingredients:
300ml lukewarm water
2 tbsp clear honey, preferably Greek
3 tbsp olive oil
400g white spelt flour
1 tbsp finely chopped fresh rosemary leaves
½ tsp salt
1¼ tsp fast-action dried yeast
75g ready-to-eat dried figs, chopped

Quantities for a large (900g) loaf
360ml water
2½ tbsp clear honey
4 tbsp olive oil
480g white spelt flour
4 tsp finely chopped fresh rosemary leaves
½ tsp salt
1½ tsp fast-action dried yeast
90g ready-to-eat dried figs

Quantities for a small (450g) loaf
180ml water
1 tbsp honey
2 tbsp olive oil
240g white spelt flour
2 tsp finely chopped fresh rosemary leaves
¼ tsp salt
¾ tsp fast-action dried yeast
45g ready-to-eat dried figs

Date and Walnut Bread

Ingredients:
75g walnut pieces
300ml semi-skimmed milk
40g butter
475g soft-grain strong white
   bread flour
40g soft light brown sugar
1 tsp salt
1 tsp fast-action dried yeast
150g ready-to-eat dried
   dates, chopped

*Quantities for a large
   (900g) loaf*
90g walnut pieces
360ml milk
50g butter
570g soft-grain strong white
   bread flour
50g soft light brown sugar
1¼ tsp salt
1¼ tsp fast-action dried
   yeast
180g ready-to-eat dried
   dates

*Quantities for a small
   (450g) loaf*
45g walnut pieces
180ml milk
25g butter
285g soft-grain strong white
   bread flour
25g soft light brown sugar
¾ tsp salt
¾ tsp fast-action dried yeast
90g ready-to eat dried dates

Date and walnuts are a classic combination; the moist texture of the dates contrasting with the crunchiness of nuts. Toast the nuts first for the best flavour and add with the dates halfway through the kneading time so that they remain in good chunky pieces.

- Put the walnuts in a small non-stick frying pan and gently toast over a low heat for 2–4 minutes, stirring or shaking the pan frequently until they smell aromatic and are just beginning to colour. Leave to cool for a few minutes.
- Meanwhile, lift the bread pan out of the bread machine and fit the kneading blade. Pour in the milk, then add the butter and about half the flour. Add the sugar, then the rest of the flour.
- Put the salt and yeast in separate corners of the pan.
- Fit the pan into the bread machine, shut the lid and set to the sweet bread setting with a light crust. Press start.
- Add the dates and nuts when the machine bleeps, or halfway through the kneading time.
- After baking, lift the pan out of the machine using oven gloves. Carefully shake out the loaf to remove it from the pan, then transfer to a wire rack, standing the loaf on its base. Leave to cool.

Baker's tip
- Don't try put the dates and nuts in the automatic dispenser if your machine has one; the dates are likely to stick and not be dispensed into the bread dough.

Spiced Almond and Apricot Loaf

This has all the sweet aromatic flavours used in Moroccan breads and pastries, including lemon, honey, almonds, cinnamon and orange flower water. Soaking the apricots for a short time before adding to the dough will help keep them moist and tender during baking.

- Put the apricots in a small bowl and sprinkle over the orange flower water. Stir, then cover with clingfilm and leave to soak.
- Meanwhile, lift the bread pan out of the bread machine and fit the kneading blade. Pour the lemon juice into a jug and make up to the 100ml mark with water. Pour into the bread pan. Add the grated lemon zest, lemon yoghurt, honey and olive or sunflower oil. Add about half of the flour, then add the ground almonds and cinnamon before adding the rest of the flour.
- Put the salt and sugar in separate corners of the pan, then make a hollow in the middle of the flour and add the yeast.
- Fit the pan into the bread machine, shut the lid and set to the sweet bread setting with a light crust. Press start.
- Add the soaked apricots when the machine bleeps, or halfway through the kneading time.
- After baking, lift the pan out of the machine using oven gloves. Carefully shake out the loaf to remove it from the pan, then transfer to a wire rack, standing the loaf on its base. Leave to cool.

Baker's tips
- If you don't have orange flower water, use orange juice instead or a blend of 2 tbsp water and ½ tsp vanilla extract.
- Plain or nut-flavoured yoghurt can be instead of the lemon yoghurt, if you prefer.
- This is not suitable for making as a large loaf.

Ingredients:
75g dried apricots, chopped
2 tbsp orange flower water
Finely grated zest and juice of 1 lemon
150ml carton lemon yoghurt
2 tbsp clear honey
2 tbsp light olive oil or sunflower oil
400g strong white bread flour
50g ground almonds
2 tsp ground cinnamon
¾ tsp salt
1 tbsp caster sugar
1¼ tsp fast-action dried yeast

Quantities for a small (450g) loaf
45g dried apricots
4 tsp orange flower water
Finely grated zest and juice of 1 small lemon (make up to 60ml with water)
90ml lemon yoghurt
20ml clear honey
20ml light olive or sunflower oil
240g strong white bread flour
30g ground almonds
1 tsp ground cinnamon
½ tsp salt
¾ tsp fast-action dried yeast

Sticky Glazed Hot Cross Bun Bread

Ingredients:
Finely grated zest and juice of 1 lemon
About 250ml water
30g butter
450g strong white bread flour
2 tbsp skimmed milk powder
2 tsp ground mixed spice
1 tsp ground ginger
50g soft light brown sugar
¾ tsp salt
1¼ tsp fast-action dried yeast
225g luxury mixed dried fruits
For the glaze
2 tbsp full-cream milk
40g caster sugar

Quantities for a small (475g) loaf
Finely grated zest and juice of 1 small lemon (make up to 180ml with water)
20g butter
270g strong white bread flour
4 tsp skimmed milk powder
1¼ tsp ground mixed spice
½ tsp ground ginger
30g soft light brown sugar
½ tsp salt
¾ tsp fast-action dried yeast
135g luxury mixed dried fruits
For the glaze
4 tsp milk
25g caster sugar

This large moist and spicy loaf is the quick and easy alternative to making and shaping individual hot cross buns and can be sliced and toasted in the same way. You can still pipe the traditional cross on top if you like, or simply leave it plain and give it a shiny sugar glaze.

- Lift the bread pan out of the bread machine and fit the kneading blade. Pour the lemon juice into a jug and make up to the 300ml mark with water. Pour into the bread pan. Add the grated lemon zest and butter. Add about half of the flour, then add the skimmed milk powder, ground spice, ginger and sugar before adding the rest of the flour.
- Put the salt and yeast in separate corners of the pan.
- Fit the pan into the bread machine, shut the lid and set to the sweet bread setting with a light crust. Press start.
- Add the fruit when the machine bleeps, or halfway through the kneading time.
- After baking, lift the pan out of the machine using oven gloves. Carefully shake out the loaf to remove it from the pan, then transfer to a wire rack, standing the loaf on its base.
- For the glaze, put the milk and sugar in a small saucepan. Heat gently, stirring until the sugar dissolves, then bring to the boil and simmer for 1 minute. Brush the warm loaf with the glaze and leave to cool.

Baker's tip
- If you want to pipe a traditional flour paste cross on top of the loaf, mix 25g plain flour in a small bowl with 2 tbsp cold water to make a thick paste. Spoon into a small polythene bag and snip off the corner. When the bread has about 20 minutes baking time left, raise the lid and pipe a cross on the top (work quickly to make sure that too much heat isn't lost). Complete baking. Glaze as before.

Fruit and Nut Bread

This heavily fruited loaf is good lightly toasted for breakfast or thickly sliced and buttered as a tea-time treat. Crunchy golden nuts and a selection of dried fruits – apricots, pears and prunes – give it both texture and moistness.

- Lift the bread pan out of the bread machine and fit the kneading blade. Stir the honey into the boiling water, then add the milk. Put the fruit in the bread pan, then pour over the liquid. Add the butter and leave the mixture to soak for 5 minutes or until lukewarm.
- Meanwhile, put the nuts in a small non-stick frying pan and cook over a low heat for 2–3 minutes or until golden and lightly toasted. Allow to cool for a minute or two.
- Add the flour and mixed spice to the bread pan. Put the salt in one of the corners of the pan, then make a shallow dip in the middle of the flour and add the yeast.
- Fit the pan into the bread machine. Put the nuts in an automatic dispenser if your machine has one. Shut the lid and set to the basic white bread setting with a light crust. Press start.
- If your machine doesn't have an automatic dispenser, add the nuts when the machine bleeps or halfway through the kneading time.
- After baking, lift the pan out of the machine using oven gloves. Carefully shake out the loaf to remove it from the pan, then transfer to a wire rack, standing the loaf on its base and leave to cool.

Baker's tip
- Check the dough towards the end of mixing. It may need an extra spoonful or two of flour, depending on the moistness of the dried fruit and how much liquid it has absorbed.

Ingredients:
175ml boiling water
3tbsp clear honey
150ml milk
50g ready-to-eat dried apricots, roughly chopped
50g ready-to-eat dried pears, roughly chopped
50g ready-to-eat dried prunes, roughly chopped
25g butter
50g chopped mixed nuts, such as almonds, cashews and hazelnuts
500g strong white bread flour
2 tsp ground mixed spice
1 tsp salt
1¼ tsp fast-action dried yeast

Quantities for a small (450g) loaf
90ml boiling water
1½ tbsp clear honey
75ml milk
25g dried apricots
25g dried pears
25g dried prunes
15g butter
25g chopped mixed nuts
250g strong white bread flour
1 tsp ground mixed spice
½ tsp salt
¾ tsp fast-action dried yeast

Shaped Breads

While most of the recipes in this book are made and baked entirely in the bread machine, there may be times when you want to bake bread in a special shape or with a filling inside. The most time-consuming stage of bread-making is mixing, kneading and proving. All this can be done using the dough programme, leaving you the fun and creative part of hand-shaping your bread. Here you'll have a chance to try some traditional international breads which were first made centuries ago, long before the invention of the bread machine, like English cottage loaf and Chelsea buns, rustic French *pain de campagne* or Italian ciabatta. Many countries and religions have special festive bread such as Danish kringle or German stollen, both served at Christmas, or poppy seed challah, enjoyed at Jewish festivals. You'll also find a selection of smaller breads here, such easy iced buns and buttery bread rolls.

Most of these recipes make standard or large loaves. Many of the doughs may be halved and made in a compact bread machine. You will need to adjust tin sizes, where applicable, and shorten cooking times a little as well, according to your manufacturer's instructions.

CHAPTER 8

Makes a large loaf

Classic Bloomer

Ingredients:
200ml full-fat milk
100ml near-boiling water
500g strong white bread
    flour plus extra for sifting
1½ tsp salt
1 tsp caster sugar
2 tsp fast-action dried yeast

This is a classic floured white loaf with a soft crust and crumb. It's fantastic when very fresh, and when a day or two old makes great toast. The dough has no additional butter or oil and only has a little sugar. The top is traditionally slashed with several deep diagonal cuts.

- Lift the bread pan out of the bread machine and fit the kneading blade. Pour in the milk and water, then add the flour.
- Put the salt and sugar in separate corners of the pan, then make a small hollow in the middle of the flour and add the yeast.
- Fit the pan into the bread machine, shut the lid and set to the dough setting. Press start.
- When the cycle is complete, turn out the risen dough and punch down to deflate. Shape the dough into a long loaf, about 25cm in length and 12cm wide, and place on a lightly greased baking sheet.
- Cover with oiled clingfilm and leave in a warm place for about 1 hour, or until doubled in size.
- Preheat the oven to 200°C/gas 6.
- Sift a fine layer of flour over the top of the loaf, then cut five deep diagonal slashes across the top.
- Bake for 35–40 minutes until golden and hollow-sounding when tapped underneath. Transfer to a wire rack to cool.

Baker's tip
- Using full-fat milk helps keep the bread soft and moist, but semi-skimmed or skimmed milk may be used if preferred.

Pain de Campagne

This rustic sourdough French bread – the name literally translates as 'country bread' – has a dark crust, traditionally slashed before baking, and a slightly chewy crumb. It is usually made with unbleached flour with a little rye or wholemeal flour to give a creamy colour.

Ingredients:
300ml sourdough starter (see page 23)
175ml lukewarm water
450g strong white bread flour, preferably unbleached
25g rye flour
1½ tsp salt
½ tsp soft light brown sugar

- Lift the bread pan out of the bread machine and fit the kneading blade. Pour in the sourdough starter and water, then add the flours, salt and sugar.
- Fit the pan into the bread machine, shut the lid and set to the dough setting. Press start.
- Check the dough when it has almost finished mixing and add a little more water if needed to make a soft dough (this will depend on the consistency of the starter).
- Turn out the risen dough and punch down to deflate. Shape the dough into a rough ball and dust with flour. Place the dough in a linen-lined proving basket, or colander lined with a well-floured linen tea towel, or shape into a round loaf and place on a floured baking sheet.
- Cover with oiled clingfilm and leave again until doubled in size, about 1½ hours.
- Towards the end of the rising time, preheat the oven to 220°C/gas 7. If you have risen the dough in a basket or colander, put a heavy baking sheet in the oven to heat for 5 minutes, then turn the dough out onto the hot baking sheet.
- Dust the loaf with flour. Cut three parallel slashes, 5mm deep, across the top of the loaf, then three more in the opposite direction.
- If you have a water spray or mister bottle, spray the oven with water to create a burst of steam. Put bread in the oven and bake for 35–40 minutes until it is a dark golden brown and sounds hollow when tapped underneath. Transfer to a wire rack to cool.

Old-fashioned Cottage Loaf

Ingredients:
300ml water
25g butter, at room
    temperature
500g plus 1 tsp strong white
    bread flour
1½ tsp salt
1 tbsp caster sugar
1¼ tsp fast-action dried
    yeast

Cottage loaves have been made in England for at least two hundred years. They are basically a large round loaf topped by a smaller one, and may have been first created as a clever way to fit more loaves in bread ovens, as they took up less floor space.

- Lift the bread pan out of the bread machine and fit the kneading blade. Pour in the water, then add the butter, followed by the 500g flour.
- Put the salt and sugar in separate corners of the pan, then make a small hollow in the middle of the flour and add the yeast.
- Fit the pan into the bread machine, shut the lid and set to the dough setting. Press start.
- When the cycle is complete, turn out the risen dough and punch down to deflate. Divide the dough into two pieces, approximately one-third and two-thirds. Shape each piece of dough into a round ball. Cover with inverted mixing bowls and leave to rise for 30 minutes.
- Transfer the larger piece to a greased baking sheet and flatten the top slightly. Using a sharp knife, cut a cross, about 4cm across, in the middle. Lightly brush with water and place the small round on top.
- Using the floured handle of a wooden spoon, push through the middle of the top round, through the second round, right down to the baking tray. Cover with oiled clingfilm and leave in a warm place to rise a little more.
- Towards the end of the proving time, preheat the oven to 200°C/gas 6.
- Sift a fine layer of flour over the top of the loaf. Bake for 35–40 minutes until golden and hollow-sounding when tapped underneath. Transfer to a wire rack to cool.

French Baguettes

French bread is unique with its crisp golden crust and airy chewy crumb. Cooked in very hot steam ovens, you can create similar conditions with a roasting tin of boiling water. Use French white flour (see page 20) for the best results.

Ingredients:
315ml lukewarm water
500g Type 55 French white flour plus extra for dusting
1½ tsp salt
1½ tsp fast-action dried yeast

- Lift the bread pan out of the bread machine and fit the kneading blade. Pour in the water, then add the flour.
- Put the salt and yeast in separate corners of the pan.
- Fit the pan into the bread machine, shut the lid and set to the dough setting. Press start.
- When the cycle is complete, turn out the risen dough and punch down to deflate. Divide the dough into three pieces. Form each into a long baguette about 30cm long (or make two longer ones if you can fit them in the oven). Place on baking sheets dusted with flour. Using a sharp knife, slash the tops with diagonal slits and brush with water. Cover with oiled clingfilm and leave to rise in a warm place for 30–40 minutes.
- Place a roasting tray of boiling water on the bottom shelf of the oven. Preheat the oven to 220°C/gas 7.
- Bake for 15 minutes. Remove the roasting tin of water and bake for a further 5 minutes for a really crisp crust. Transfer to a wire rack to cool. Serve slightly warm or cold. These are best eaten on the same day.

Baker's tips
- Baguettes are traditionally baked in baguette trays: baguette-shaped tins which are perforated to give a crisp crust and give the bread the familiar round shape. Home-baked loaves will have a flat base.
- You can use cornmeal for dusting if you prefer.

Focaccia with Fresh Rosemary

Ingredients:
300ml water
5 tbsp olive oil
475g strong white bread
   flour
1½ tsp salt
1 tsp fast-action dried yeast
4 large sprigs fresh rosemary
Sea salt flakes

- Lift the bread pan out of the bread machine and fit the kneading blade. Pour in the water, then add 3 tbsp of the oil and the flour.
- Put the salt and yeast in separate corners of the pan.
- Fit the pan into the bread machine, shut the lid and set to the dough setting. Press start.
- When the cycle is complete, turn out the risen dough and punch down to deflate. Roll out the dough to a 25cm round. Grease a 28cm metal flan tin and place on a lightly greased baking sheet and put the dough in the middle, then push the dough to the edges using your fingertips. Loosely cover with oiled clingfilm and leave in a warm place to rise for 30 minutes or until well risen.
- Using the end of a wooden spoon dipped in flour, make deep dimples all over the dough. Brush the top with the remaining 2 tbsp olive oil. Divide the rosemary into smaller sprigs and poke in the holes. Sprinkle with sea salt flakes. Re-cover the focaccia with the clingfilm and leave to rise for a further 5 minutes.
- Preheat the oven to 200°C/gas 6.
- If you have a water spray, spray the top of the loaf with water (this will help keep the crust soft). Bake for 20–25 minutes until firm and golden (don't overcook, the crust should be a very light, not dark in colour). Transfer to a wire rack, lift off the flan tin and leave to cool.

Baker's tip
- The flan ring is an easy way to keep the focaccia a perfect round shape, but if you don't have one, simply roll the dough into a 25cm round and cook on the baking sheet. Alternatively, you can use a banneton; traditionally a linen-lined wicker basket in which the loaf is left to rise, providing it with shape before it is turned out onto the baking sheet. Nowadays, these are available in silicone and plastic and a variety of shapes, including oval and rectangular.

Makes two 350g **loaves**

Italian Ciabatta

Ciabatta means 'slipper' in Italian and describes these flattish oval loaves. The bread has a lovely light texture and crisp crust and is flavoured with olive oil. Sliced in half lengthways, they make great open sandwiches, topped with Italian deli meats and sliced plum tomatoes.

Ingredients:
150ml lukewarm water
300ml sourdough starter (see page 23)
2 tbsp virgin olive oil
350g strong white bread flour
1½ tsp salt
½ tsp fast-action dried yeast

- Lift the bread pan out of the bread machine and fit the kneading blade. Pour in the water, then add the sourdough starter and the oil. Top with the flour.
- Put the salt and yeast in separate corners of the pan.
- Fit the pan into the bread machine, shut the lid and set to the dough setting. Press start.
- When the cycle is complete, turn out the risen dough into a large oiled bowl (it will be quite soft and sticky). Cover loosely with oiled clingfilm and leave in a warm place for about 1 hour or until more than doubled in size (this extra rising gives the bread a light, airy texture).
- Lightly dust two baking sheets with flour. Punch bake the dough to deflate, then turn out onto a lightly floured surface. Cut the dough in half and shape each piece into a long oval. Place on the baking sheet, cover with oiled clingfilm and leave to rise for about 30 minutes.
- Towards the end of rising time, preheat the oven to 200°C/gas 6. Carefully remove the clingfilm and bake for 20–25 minutes or until dark golden and hollow-sounding when tapped.
- Transfer the loaves to a wire rack and leave to cool.

Baker's tips
- For a truly authentic result, use Italian Type 00 bread flour.
- For olive and salami ciabatta, reduce the salt in the dough to 1 tsp and add 1½ tsp dried oregano with the flour. Knead 40g finely chopped salami and 40g chopped stoned black olives into the dough after the second rising and before shaping into loaves.

Pesto and Pine Nut Stromboli

Ingredients:
225ml lukewarm water
3 tbsp olive oil plus extra for
brushing
350g strong white bread
flour
½ tsp salt
1 tsp fast-action dried yeast

For the filling
100g pine nuts
150g Mozzarella cheese,
coarsely grated
75g Parmesan, finely grated
3 tbsp pesto
Freshly ground black pepper
Pinch of sea salt flakes, for
sprinkling

This is named after a volcanic island near Italy because the filling erupts through holes in the crust. The pesto, pine nut and cheese filling is rolled inside the dough, so appears in an attractive spiral when sliced. It is best served warm while the cheese is still meltingly soft.

- Lift the bread pan out of the bread machine and fit the kneading blade. Pour in the water, add the olive oil, then add the flour.
- Put the salt in a corner of the pan, then make a small hollow in the middle of the flour and add the yeast.
- Fit the pan into the bread machine, shut the lid and set to the dough setting. Press start.
- While the dough is being prepared, make the filling. Toast the pine nuts in a small non-stick frying pan over a low heat for 3–4 minutes or until just beginning to colour, then tip into a bowl and leave to cool.
- Add the Mozzarella and Parmesan cheeses, the pesto and a little freshly ground black pepper. Stir everything together.
- When the cycle is complete, turn out the risen dough onto a lightly floured surface and punch down to deflate. Cover with a tea towel and leave to rest for 10 minutes.
- Roll out the dough to a 35 x 25cm rectangle. Scatter and spread with the filling to within 1cm of the edges, then roll up from one of the short ends and place join-side down on a large, lightly greased baking sheet.
- Loosely cover with oiled clingfilm and leave in a warm place for 30-40 minutes until well risen.
- Towards the end of proving, preheat the oven to 200°C/gas 6.
- Using a large skewer, pierce about 15 holes at regular intervals all over the top of the dough, going right through to the baking tray. Lightly brush the top with olive oil and sprinkle with sea salt flakes.
- Bake for 30–35 minutes or until well risen and golden. Leave on the baking tray for a few minutes, then transfer to a wire rack. Serve warm or cool.

Makes 18 rolls

Buttery Bread Rolls

These small buttery egg-enriched bread rolls are fantastic for feeding a crowd at picnics or dinner parties. They are based on the German partybrot, individual rolls baked together in a round tin so the tops and bases are deliciously crisp, but the sides and centres stay soft.

Ingredients:
250ml milk
50g butter
2 eggs, lightly beaten
500g strong white bread
 flour
1½ tsp salt
2 tbsp caster sugar
2 tsp fast-action dried
 yeast
Sesame and poppy seeds,
 for sprinkling

- Pour about half the milk into a small pan. Add the butter and gently heat until the butter has melted. Stir in the rest of the milk.
- Lift the bread pan out of the bread machine and fit the kneading blade. Pour in the milk and butter mixture. Reserve 1 tbsp of the beaten egg, then add the rest of the eggs to the pan, followed by the flour. Put the salt and sugar in separate corners of the pan, then make a hollow in the middle of the flour and add the yeast.
- Fit the pan into the bread machine, shut the lid and set to the dough setting. Press start.
- When the cycle is complete, turn out the risen dough and punch down to deflate. Leave to rest for 5 minutes, then divide the dough into 18 equal pieces. Shape each into a round ball.
- Grease a round 24cm tin and arrange 11 of the rolls around the edges. Arrange an inner ring of 6 rolls, then place one in the middle. Cover with oiled clingfilm and leave to rise for about 40 minutes or until doubled in size.
- Preheat the oven to 200°C/gas 6. Brush the tops of the rolls with the reserved beaten egg and sprinkle some with sesame seeds, some with poppy seeds and leave a few plain.
- Bake for 35–40 minutes or until dark golden. Turn out on a wire rack and cover with a tea towel to keep the bread soft. Serve warm or cold.

Bagels

Ingredients:
200ml warm water
2 tbsp sunflower oil
3 medium eggs
450g very strong white
   bread flour
1½ tsp salt
1 tbsp caster sugar
2 tsp fast-action dried yeast

These tasty little breads, Jewish in origin, are great teamed up with all sorts of fillings, from cream cheese and smoked salmon to meat and liver pâtés. To create the unique, chewy crust, they are double-cooked, first by briefly poaching, then baking in a hot oven.

- Lift the bread pan out of the bread machine and fit the kneading blade. Pour in the water, then add the oil. Lightly whisk 2 of the eggs and add to the pan, followed by the flour.
- Put the salt and sugar in separate corners of the pan, then make a small hollow in the middle of the flour and add the yeast.
- Fit the pan into the bread machine, shut the lid and set to the dough setting. Press start.
- When the cycle is complete, turn out the risen dough onto a lightly floured surface and punch down to deflate. Divide the dough into 12 pieces. Form each into a 20cm long sausage shape, dampen the ends, then curve into a ring and pinch the edges together.
- Put on a lightly greased baking sheet, cover with oiled clingfilm and leave in a warm place for about 1 hour, or until slightly risen and puffy.
- Preheat the oven to 200°C/gas 6.
- Bring a large pan of lightly salted water to the boil. Drop the bagels into the water, one at a time, and poach for 20 seconds. Lift out with a large draining spoon and return to the baking sheet.
- Lightly whisk the remaining egg and brush over the bagels to glaze. Bake for 14–15 minutes or until dark golden brown. Transfer to a wire rack to cool.
- When cold, store in an airtight container.

Baker's tips

- The bagels can be finished with a variety of toppings. After brushing with egg, sprinkle with sesame, poppy or caraway seeds.
- For rye bagels, substitute 100g of the white bread flour for rye flour and use 1 tbsp malt extract in the dough instead of caster sugar. Sprinkle the tops with caraway seeds.
- For cinnamon raisin bagels, add $1\frac{1}{2}$ tsp ground cinnamon and an extra 1 tbsp sugar to the dough and reduce the salt to 1 tsp. Soak 50g raisins in 1 tbsp orange juice or water and add to the dough when the machine bleeps or halfway through the kneading time.

Chelsea Buns

Ingredients:

For the dough
200ml lukewarm milk
50g butter, at room
   temperature
1 medium egg, lightly
   beaten
450g strong white bread
   flour
25g caster sugar
1 tsp salt
1 tsp fast-action dried yeast

For the filling
50g butter, at room
   temperature
25g caster sugar
50g almonds or hazelnuts,
   chopped
1 tsp ground mixed spice
Finely grated zest of 1
   lemon or 1 orange
50g sultanas
50g currants

For the glaze
50g caster sugar
5 tbsp water
2 tsp orange flower water
   (optional)

Chelsea buns were created at The Bun House of Chelsea in the 17th century. This follows the traditional filling of dried fruit, nuts and spices but you can vary the filling if you prefer. The buns should be very dark golden and crisp, so don't undercook them.

- Lift the bread pan out of the bread machine and fit the kneading blade. Pour in the milk, then add the butter and beaten egg. Add half the flour, then add the sugar, then the rest of the flour.
- Put the salt in a corner of the bread pan, then make a shallow dip in the middle of the flour and add the yeast.
- Fit the pan into the bread machine, shut the lid and set to the dough setting. Press start.
- While the dough is being prepared, make the filling. Cream the butter with 15g of the sugar. Mix together the rest of the sugar, nuts, spice, grated zest and dried fruit.
- When the dough cycle is complete, turn out the risen dough onto a lightly floured surface and punch down to deflate. Cover with a tea towel and leave to rest for 2–3 minutes. Meanwhile, grease a 23 x 28cm tin (a roasting tin is fine) with unsalted butter or sunflower oil.
- Roll out the dough to a square of about 30cm. Dot the creamed mixture evenly all over the dough, leaving a clear 2cm rim all the way round. Fold the dough in half and roll out to the same size as before. Scatter the fruit and spice mixture over the dough, leaving a border as before. Roll up the dough and place on a board with the seam underneath.
- With a sharp knife, cut into 12 even-sized pieces. Arrange cut-side up in the prepared tin, spacing them out evenly.
- Cover the tin loosely with oiled clingfilm and leave in a warm place to rise for about 20 minutes or until the buns have doubled in size and are touching each other.

- Towards the end of the proving time, preheat the oven to 200°C/gas 6.
- Bake for 25–30 minutes or until well risen and very dark golden, covering the top with foil towards the end if it starts to over-brown. Leave in the tin for 10 minutes, then carefully turn out onto a wire rack.
- To make the glaze, put the sugar and water in a small saucepan. Heat gently until dissolved, stirring occasionally, then bring to the boil. Simmer for 2–3 minutes until thick and syrupy. Cool for a few minutes, then stir in the orange flower water, if using. Brush the syrup over the buns while still warm. Serve warm.

Poppy Seed Challah

Ingredients:
200ml water
2 tbsp clear honey
60g butter
2 eggs, lightly beaten
500g strong white bread
    flour
½ tsp salt
2 tsp fast-action dried yeast
2–3 tsp poppy seeds

This plaited loaf, enriched with eggs, butter and honey, is the traditional Jewish Festival and Sabbath bread. Its name means 'offering' in Hebrew and the three braids symbolise truth, peace and justice, while the poppy seeds represent the manna that fell from heaven.

- Lift the bread pan out of the bread machine and fit the kneading blade. Pour about half the water into a small pan. Add the honey and butter and heat gently until the butter has just melted and the mixture is warm. Pour into the bread pan and add the rest of the water. Reserve 1 tbsp of the beaten egg, then add the rest to the bread pan, followed by the flour.
- Put the salt in a corner of the bread pan, then make a shallow dip in the middle of the flour and add the yeast.
- Fit the pan into the bread machine, shut the lid and set to the dough setting. Press start.
- When the dough cycle is complete, turn out the risen dough onto a lightly floured surface and punch down to deflate.
- Divide the dough into three equal pieces. Roll out each piece with your hands to form a 15cm long rope. Use the flattened palms of your hands to taper the ends of the rope, so that it is slightly thinner at the ends than the middle. Plait the three pieces together, moistening and tightly pressing the ends to seal.
- Place on a lightly greased baking sheet, tucking about 2cm of the ends under to make a neat shape. Cover with oiled clingfilm and leave in a warm place for about 45 minutes, until doubled in size.
- Towards the end of the proving time, preheat the oven to 180°C/gas 4.
- Remove the clingfilm and brush the loaf with the reserved beaten egg, then sprinkle with poppy seeds as thickly or sparsely as you like.

- Bake for 40–45 minutes until a rich golden brown and hollow-sounding when tapped underneath. Cool on a wire rack.

Baker's tip
- To make a coiled challah (traditionally baked for the Jewish New Year), roll the dough with the palms of your hands to a rope about 40cm long, tapering the ends. Coil into a snail-like spiral, tucking the end under the coil. Bake as before.

Kringle

Ingredients:

For the dough
150ml milk
50g butter, at room
    temperature
1 medium egg, lightly
    beaten
350g strong white bread
    flour
25g caster sugar
Seeds from 6 cardamom
    pods, lightly crushed
Finely grated zest of 2
    lemons
½ tsp salt
2 tsp fast-action dried yeast

For the filling
50g butter
50g caster sugar
2 tsp ground cinnamon

For the icing
100g icing sugar
1 tbsp lemon juice

In this Danish Christmas treat, the dough is flavoured with lemon and cardamom, filled with cinnamon butter, then shaped into a huge pretzel; the Danish sign for a bakery. This is a simplified version of the recipe, which usually involves hours of layering butter between the dough.

- Lift the bread pan out of the bread machine and fit the kneading blade. Pour in the milk, then add the butter. Set aside 1 tbsp of beaten egg, then add the rest to the bread pan. Add about half the flour, then add the sugar, crushed cardamom seeds and lemon zest. Top with the rest of the flour.
- Put the salt in a corner of the bread pan, then make a shallow dip in the middle of the flour and add the yeast.
- Fit the pan into the bread machine, shut the lid and set to the dough setting. Press start.
- While the dough is being prepared, make the filling. Mix the butter, sugar and cinnamon together until soft and creamy.
- When the dough cycle is complete, turn out the risen dough onto a lightly floured surface and punch down to deflate. Cover with a tea towel and leave to rest for 2–3 minutes. Meanwhile, grease a large baking sheet or line it with baking parchment.
- Roll out the dough to a rectangle about 40 x 15cm. Spread the creamed ingredients evenly all over the dough, leaving a 2cm border around the edge. Brush water along one long edge, then roll up the dough from the other long edge. Press firmly along the join.
- Shape the dough into a large pretzel knot and place on the baking sheet, tucking both ends under. Loosely cover with oiled clingfilm and leave to rise in a warm place for about 40 minutes until doubled in size.

- When the bread is nearly ready to cook, preheat the oven to 200°C/gas 6.
- Remove the clingfilm and brush with the reserved beaten egg. Bake for 25–30 minutes or until dark golden brown and hollow-sounding when tapped underneath. Transfer to a wire rack to cool.
- When the bread is cool, make the icing. Sift the icing sugar into a small bowl and stir in the lemon juice to make a fairly thick icing. Drizzle over the loaf and leave to set before serving.

Stollen

Ingredients:
200ml milk
50g butter
350g strong white bread flour
40g golden caster sugar
1 tsp salt
2 tsp fast-action dried yeast
100g mixed dried fruit
25g chopped candied peel or mixed peel
200g almond paste
1 tbsp icing sugar, to dust

This traditional German fruit bread is served at Christmas and makes a great alternative to a rich fruit cake – the almond paste filling represents baby Jesus wrapped in swaddling clothes. There's a simplified version of stollen, made entirely in the breadmaker on page 94.

- Lift the bread pan out of the bread machine and fit the kneading blade. Pour about half the milk into a small pan. Add the butter and heat gently until the butter has just melted and the mixture is warm. Add the rest of the milk, then pour into the bread pan. Add about half of the flour, then add the sugar followed by the rest of the flour.
- Put the salt in a corner of the bread pan, then make a shallow dip in the middle of the flour and add the yeast.
- Put the dried fruit and peel in the automatic dispenser if your machine has one.
- Fit the pan into the bread machine, shut the lid and set to the dough setting. Press start.
- If you don't have an automatic dispenser or it isn't large enough to take this quantity of fruit, add the fruit and peel halfway through the kneading time or when the machine bleeps.
- When the dough cycle is complete, turn out the risen dough onto a lightly floured surface and punch down to deflate. Cover with a clean tea towel and leave to rest for 3–4 minutes.
- Roll the dough into a rectangle about 25 x 20cm. Roll the almond paste on a surface lightly dusted with icing sugar to a sausage shape slightly shorter than the dough. Place in the middle of the dough, then fold in the two shorter edges over the marzipan. Fold over one long edge, then the other.
- Place on a lightly greased baking sheet with the join facing down. Cover with oiled clingfilm and leave in a warm place for about 45 minutes until doubled in size.

- Towards the end of the proving time, preheat the oven to 180°C/gas 4.
- Bake the stollen for 35–40 minutes or until golden brown and hollow-sounding when tapped underneath. Transfer to wire rack and dust with icing sugar. Serve hot or cold.

Baker's tip
- Yellow almond paste (marzipan) is traditionally used rather than white, but either is fine. Instead of bought almond paste, you can make your own by stirring 65g golden caster sugar and 65g ground almonds into a beaten egg. This will make a very soft almond paste which you should spread down the middle of the dough.

serves 6

Sticky Syrup-soaked Savarin

Ingredients:

For the dough
125ml milk
50g butter
2 medium eggs, lightly
   beaten
200g strong white bread
   flour
Pinch of salt
1 tbsp golden caster sugar
1½ tsp fast-action dried
   yeast

For the rum syrup
100g golden caster sugar
5 tbsp water
3 tbsp dark rum

For the filling
450g strawberries, hulled
   and halved
1 tbsp lemon juice
1 tbsp golden caster sugar
300ml double or whipping
   cream

This delectable dessert is a sponge-like yeasted cake, drenched in a rich, boozy syrup and served piled high with fresh fruit and cream. Traditionally made with dark rum (rum babas are mini versions), you can use a different spirit or liqueur, or make it alcohol free.

- Lift the bread pan out of the bread machine and fit the kneading blade. Pour about half the milk into a small pan. Add the butter and heat gently until the butter has just melted and the mixture is warm. Add the rest of the milk, then pour into the bread pan, followed by the eggs. Add the flour.
- Put the salt and sugar in separate corners of the bread pan, then make a shallow dip in the middle of the flour and add the yeast.
- Fit the pan into the bread machine, shut the lid and set to the dough setting. Press start.
- When the dough cycle is complete, the dough will be very soft and sticky. Gently stir with a rubber spatula, then spoon and scrape into a well-greased 25cm ring mould. Cover with oiled clingfilm and leave to rise in a warm place for about an hour until the mixture has risen to within 1cm of the top of the tin.
- When almost ready, preheat the oven to 200°C/gas 6.
- Remove the clingfilm and bake for 20 minutes or until well risen and golden. Leave in the tin for a few minutes, then turn out onto a wire rack and leave to cool for 10 minutes.
- While the savarin is baking, make the rum syrup. Put the sugar and water in a small saucepan and heat gently, stirring occasionally until the sugar has dissolved. Increase the heat a little and bubble for 1–2 minutes. Remove from the heat, leave to cool for 10 minutes, then stir in the rum.
- Place a large plate under the rack to catch drips, then carefully spoon the syrup over the warm savarin. Spoon over any syrup that collects on the plate underneath. Carefully transfer to a serving plate and allow to cool.

- For the filling, sprinkle the strawberries with lemon juice and sugar and gently stir to coat. Lightly whip the cream until soft peaks form, then pile into the centre of the savarin. Top with the strawberries and serve.

Baker's tips
- You can use an orange liqueur instead of the rum, if preferred, or try cherry brandy and fill the centre with stoned fresh cherries instead of strawberries.
- For a summer fruit savarin, use 2 tsp rosewater instead of the rum. Whip the cream with 1 tsp vanilla extract and use a mixture of soft red fruits such as raspberries, redcurrants and small strawberries.

Raisin Loaf

Popular in America as a breakfast or brunch bread, this classic bake has a stunning spiral of buttery cinnamon sugar and plump raisins – traditionally Californian ones – in every slice. You can make a simplified version entirely in the breadmaker if you prefer.

Ingredients:
150ml semi-skimmed or skimmed milk
40g butter, at room temperature
1 medium egg, lightly beaten
350g strong white bread flour
50g caster sugar
½ tsp salt
1½ tsp fast-action dried yeast

For the filling
100g raisins
1 tbsp boiling water
25g butter, softened
25g soft light brown sugar
2 tsp ground cinnamon
1 tbsp milk
1 tbsp demerara sugar

- Lift the bread pan out of the bread machine and fit the kneading blade. Pour in the milk, then add the butter and beaten egg. Add half the flour, then add the sugar, then the rest of the flour.
- Put the salt in a corner of the bread pan, then make a shallow dip in the middle of the flour and add the yeast.
- Fit the pan into the bread machine, shut the lid and set to the dough setting. Press start.
- While the dough is being prepared, put the raisins in a small bowl and drizzle over the boiling water. Stir to coat all the raisins, then cover with clingfilm and leave to soak for about an hour until the dough is made.
- When the dough cycle is complete, turn out the risen dough onto a lightly floured surface and punch down to deflate. Cover with a tea towel and leave to rest for about 5 minutes.
- Meanwhile, grease a 900g loaf tin. Beat the butter, sugar and cinnamon together. Stir in the raisins.
- Roll out the dough to a rectangle 30cm long with the width 2cm shorter than the loaf tin. Dot the filling all over the dough, spreading out as much as possible (there will be bare patches, so just try to divide the filling as evenly as you can). Starting from a short end, roll up the dough and place in the tin with the seam underneath.
- Cover the tin loosely with oiled clingfilm and leave in a warm place to rise for about an hour or until the dough has risen to the top of the tin.
- Preheat the oven to 200°C/gas 6.

- When the dough is slightly higher than the top of the tin, brush the top with milk and sprinkle with demerara sugar.
- Bake for 30–35 minutes or until well risen and dark golden, covering the top with foil if it starts to over-brown. Leave in the tin for a few minutes, then turn out and cool on a wire rack.

Baker's tip
- You can make this entirely in a bread machine, but the fruit and cinnamon filling will be mixed into the loaf rather than in a swirl. Just use 40g butter (leaving out the extra 25g butter and 25g soft light brown sugar in the filling). Put the milk, butter and egg in the bread pan. Add about half of the flour, then the caster sugar, soaked raisins and cinnamon. Top with the rest of the flour. Put the salt and yeast in separate corners of the pan and set to the sweet bread setting. Press start. Add the soaked raisins when the machine bleeps or halfway through the kneading time.

Easy Iced Buns

Ingredients:
225ml milk
1 tsp vanilla extract
15g butter
1 egg, lightly beaten
450g strong white bread
    flour
75g caster sugar
½ tsp salt
1½ tsp fast-action dried
    yeast

For the icing
75g icing sugar, sifted
2–3 tsp fresh orange juice,
    lemon juice or water

These long oval-shaped sweet buns appear in every baker's shop window, usually topped with a thick white or garish pink icing. For a slightly healthier finish and avoiding artificial colouring, here the icing is made with fresh orange or lemon juice instead.

- Lift the bread pan out of the bread machine and fit the kneading blade. Pour in the milk, then add the vanilla, butter and beaten egg.
- Add half the flour, then add the sugar, then the rest of the flour. Put the salt in a corner of the bread pan, then make a shallow dip in the middle of the flour and add the yeast.
- Fit the pan into the bread machine, shut the lid and set to the dough setting. Press start.
- When the dough cycle is complete, turn out the risen dough onto a lightly floured surface and punch down to deflate. Cover with a tea towel and leave to rest for about 5 minutes.
- Grease a large baking sheet or line with baking parchment. Divide the dough into 8 even-sized pieces. Shape each into an oval finger shape. Place on the baking sheet, spacing them at least 2cm apart. Cover loosely with oiled clingfilm and leave to rise in a warm place for about 30 minutes or until doubled in size.
- When nearly ready, preheat the oven to 200°C/gas 6.
- Bake the buns for about 12 minutes until risen and pale golden. Lift onto a wire rack and leave to cool.
- Put the icing sugar in a bowl and stir in 2 tsp juice or water, adding a little more if necessary to make a smooth, fairly thick icing. Drizzle over the top of the buns and leave for a few minutes to set before serving.

Baker's tip
- You can make a natural pink icing by squeezing the juice from 2–3 raspberries through a tea strainer and mixing with the icing sugar. Add a little water if necessary.

Serves 8–10

Creamy Chocolate Braid

Here is a rich chocolate bread dough which contains both plain chocolate and cocoa powder, is filled with a smooth and creamy centre before baking. Left to cool before slicing, a thick dusting of icing sugar with just a little ground cinnamon adds the perfect finishing touch.

- Lift the bread pan out of the bread machine and fit the kneading blade. Pour in the milk, then add the chocolate and butter. Leave for 5 minutes or until the mixture is barely warm and the chocolate and butter are very soft and almost melted.
- Add the beaten egg, followed by about half the flour. Top with the cocoa powder and sugar, then the rest of the flour. Put the salt in a corner of the bread pan, then make a shallow dip in the middle of the flour and add the yeast.
- Fit the pan into the bread machine, shut the lid and set to the dough setting. Press start.
- When the dough is almost ready, make the filling. Mix the cream cheese, almonds, egg yolk, icing sugar and vanilla together.
- Turn out the dough on a lightly floured surface and knead until smooth. Roll out to a rectangle 30x25cm. Spread the filling in a 10cm-wide strip lengthways down the middle of the dough to within 5cm of each end.
- Make diagonal cuts down the side of the dough at about 1.5cm intervals. Fold both ends of the dough up and over the filling, then fold alternate left and right strips over one another into the middle.
- Place on a greased baking tray and loosely cover with oiled clingfilm. Leave to rise in a warm place for about 45 minutes, or until almost doubled in size. Towards the end of the proving time, preheat the oven to 200°C/gas 6.
- Brush with lightly beaten egg white and bake for 20–25 minutes or until well-risen and firm. Cool on a wire rack. Lightly dust with icing sugar, then dust with the cinnamon, then again with a little more icing sugar. Slice and serve.

Ingredients:

For the dough
200ml hot milk
75g plain chocolate, roughly chopped
50g butter, at room temperature, cubed
1 medium egg, lightly beaten
400g strong white bread flour
50g cocoa powder
25g caster sugar
1 tsp salt
1¼ tsp fast-action dried yeast

For the filling
200g full-fat cream cheese, at room temperature
50g ground almonds
1 egg, separated
50g icing sugar, sifted, plus extra for dusting
1 tsp vanilla extract
½ tsp ground cinnamon

Breads for Special Diets

Your passion for baking can also be good for your health; bread is one of the most versatile sources of starchy carbohydrate and also provides many vitamins and minerals. When it comes to baking breads for those on special diets, the breadmaker excels. As well as extra-nutritious breads such as Breakfast Bread and Egg-enriched White Bread, you'll find several loaves here to suit those who have food intolerances to wheat and gluten; both basic white and brown breads and other more adventurous flavours such as cheese and sun-dried tomato and chilli corn and polenta.

You'll also find a delicious Gluten-free Citrus Cake on page 157.

CHAPTER 9

Breakfast Bread

Ingredients:
75g no-added sugar muesli
150ml hot milk
200ml hot water
2 tbsp sunflower oil
25g wheatgerm
425g strong white bread
    flour
1 tsp salt
2 tsp soft light brown sugar
1½ tsp fast-action dried yeast

*Quantities for a large (900g)
    loaf*
90g muesli
180ml hot milk
240ml hot water
2 tbsp plus 1 tsp sunflower
    oil
30g wheatgerm
510g strong white bread
    flour
1¾ tsp salt
2½ tsp soft light brown
    sugar
2 tsp fast-action dried yeast

*Quantities for a small (450g)
    loaf*
45g muesli
90ml hot milk
120ml hot water
1 tbsp sunflower oil
15g wheatgerm
255g strong white bread flour
¾ tsp salt
1¼ tsp soft light brown sugar
¾ tsp fast-action dried yeast

Choose muesli with no added sugar and a good proportion of nuts and grains, such as wheat and oat flakes. Wheatgerm adds a great texture and is also high in protein and packed with vitamins including folic acid. For best results, allow the time to soak and soften the muesli.

- Lift the bread pan out of the bread machine and fit the kneading blade. Put the muesli in the bread pan and pour over the hot milk and water. Add the oil and allow to stand for 10 minutes until the muesli is soft and the mixture is lukewarm.
- Add the wheatgerm and flour. Put the salt and sugar in separate corners of the pan, then make a shallow dip in the middle of the flour and add the yeast.
- Fit the pan into the bread machine, shut the lid and set to the basic white setting with a crust of your choice. Press start.
- After baking, lift the pan out of the machine using oven gloves. Carefully shake out the loaf to remove it from the pan, then transfer to a wire rack, standing the loaf on its base. Leave to cool.

Baker's tip
- Check the dough during mixing and add a little more water if the dough looks too dry, as some brands of muesli may absorb more than others.
- This is a good source of folic acid – vital in the early months of pregnancy.

Makes a 750g loaf

Egg-enriched White Bread

As well as protein, eggs provide useful amounts of vitamins A, B_2, B_{12}, niacin and E, iron and zinc. This bread also contains skimmed milk powder for extra protein and calcium. It's great for vegetarians, or to make a simple meal such as vegetable soup more nutritious.

- Lift the bread pan out of the bread machine and fit the kneading blade. Whisk the eggs in a jug, then pour in enough cold water to come up to the 325ml mark. Pour into the bread pan. Add the oil, followed by the flour and skimmed milk powder.
- Put the salt and sugar in separate corners of the pan, then make a shallow dip in the middle of the flour and add the yeast.
- Fit the pan into the bread machine, shut the lid and set to the basic white setting with a crust of your choice. Press start.
- After baking, lift the pan out of the machine using oven gloves. Carefully shake out the loaf to remove it from the pan, then transfer to a wire rack, standing the loaf on its base. Leave to cool.

Baker's tips
- This loaf is high in protein.
- If preferred, you can substitute 200g of the white bread flour with 200g wholemeal or brown bread flour. You will need to add an extra tablespoon of water as well.

Ingredients:
2 eggs
About 220ml water
1½ tbsp sunflower oil
500g strong white bread flour
2 tbsp skimmed milk powder
1½ tsp salt
4 tsp caster sugar
1½ tsp fast-action dried yeast

Quantities for a large (900g) loaf
2 eggs plus enough water to make 390ml
2 tbsp sunflower oil
600g strong white bread flour
2½ tbsp skimmed milk powder
1¾ tsp salt
5 tsp caster sugar
1½ tsp fast-action dried yeast

Quantities for a small (375g) loaf
1 egg plus enough water to make 195ml
1 tbsp sunflower oil
300g strong white bread flour
1 tbsp plus 1 tsp skimmed milk powder
¾ tsp salt
2½ tsp caster sugar
¾ tsp fast-action dried yeast

Extra-healthy White

Ingredients:
300ml water
2 tbsp sunflower oil
40g quinoa flakes
25g wheat germ
425g strong white bread
    flour
2 tbsp skimmed milk powder
1 tsp salt
2 tbsp clear honey
1 tsp fast-action dried yeast

*Quantities for a large (900g)
    loaf*
360ml water
2½ tbsp sunflower oil
50g quinoa flakes
30g wheat germ
510g strong white bread
    flour
4 tsp skimmed milk powder
1¼ tsp salt
2½ tbsp clear honey
1¼ tsp fast-action dried
    yeast

*Quantities for a small (450g)
    loaf*
180ml water
1 tbsp sunflower oil
25g quinoa flakes
15g wheat germ
250g strong white bread
    flour
2 tsp skimmed milk powder
¾ tsp salt
1 tbsp clear honey
¾ tsp fast-action dried yeast

For those who prefer white bread to wholemeal or brown, this loaf contains added protein, vitamins and minerals from skimmed milk powder, quinoa flakes and wheatgerm. If you like, you can use skimmed milk instead of water to increase the amount of calcium as well.

- Lift the bread pan out of the bread machine and fit the kneading blade. Pour in the water, then add the oil, followed by the quinoa and wheat germ. Add about half of the flour, then sprinkle over the skimmed milk powder. Top with the rest of the flour.
- Put the salt and honey in separate corners of the pan (but don't let the honey drizzle down the side of the pan as it may stick and burn), then make a shallow dip in the middle and add the yeast.
- Fit the pan into the bread machine, shut the lid and set to the basic white setting with the crust of your choice. Press start.
- After baking, lift the pan out of the machine using oven gloves. Carefully shake out the loaf to remove it from the pan, then transfer to a wire rack, standing the loaf on its base. Leave to cool.

Baker's tip
- Quinoa contains all eight amino acids, so is a useful source of protein. Wheatgerm is high in protein and contains numerous vitamins and minerals including a good amount of vitamin E.

Multi-seed Buckwheat Bread

Although the name suggests otherwise, buckwheat is not a member of the wheat family. The triangular-shaped grains make a creamy-coloured flour. It does have a strong flavour so is best used in small amounts and combined with other flours when bread-making.

- Lift the bread pan out of the bread machine and fit the kneading blade. Pour in the water, eggs, oil and vinegar. Add about half of the wheat-and gluten-free flour, then add the buckwheat flour and seeds. Top with the rest of the flour.
- Put the sugar and salt in separate corners of the pan, then make a hollow in the middle and add the yeast.
- Fit the pan into the bread machine, shut the lid and set to the gluten-free, rapid setting with a crust of your choice. Press start.
- After baking, lift the pan out of the machine using oven gloves. Carefully shake out the loaf to remove it from the pan, then transfer to a wire rack, standing the loaf on its base. Leave to cool.

Baker's tips
- This is suitable for many people on a wheat-free diet. Buckwheat flour contains a small amount of gluten, so is suitable for those who find eating large amounts difficult, but not for those with coeliac disease.
- This is not suitable for making as a larger loaf.

Ingredients:
300ml lukewarm water
2 medium eggs, lightly beaten
4 tbsp sunflower oil
1 tsp wine vinegar
300g wheat- and gluten-free bread flour with natural gum
100g buckwheat flour
2 tbsp sunflower seeds
2 tbsp pumpkin seeds
1 tbsp sesame seeds
1 tbsp poppy seeds
2 tbsp soft light brown sugar
1 tsp salt
2 tsp fast-action dried yeast

Quantities for a small (375g) loaf
150ml lukewarm water
1 medium egg
2 tbsp sunflower oil
½ tsp wine vinegar
150g wheat- and gluten-free bread flour
50g buckwheat flour
1 tbsp sunflower seeds
1 tbsp pumpkin seeds
1½ tsp sesame seeds
1½ tsp poppy seeds
1 tbsp soft light brown sugar
½ tsp salt
1 tsp fast-action dried yeast

Wholewheat Spelt Bread

Ingredients:
350ml water
2 tbsp olive oil
500g wholewheat spelt flour
1 tsp salt
1 tbsp honey
1¼ tsp fast-action dried
   yeast

Quantities for a large (900g)
   loaf
425ml water
2 tbsp olive oil
600g wholewheat spelt flour
1¼ tsp salt
4 tsp honey
1½ tsp fast-action dried
   yeast

Quantities for a small (450g)
   loaf
215ml water
1 tbsp olive oil
300g wholewheat spelt flour
¾ tsp salt
2 tsp honey
¾ tsp fast-action dried yeast

Spelt is a variety of wheat that has been grown and milled for centuries, and this is similar to bread enjoyed by the Ancient Romans, although not made in a machine! While unsuitable for those on a gluten-free diet, it can be tolerated by many who can't eat common wheat.

- Lift the bread pan out of the bread machine and fit the kneading blade. Pour the water into the bread pan. Add the oil, followed by the flour.
- Put the salt and honey in separate corners of the pan (but don't let the honey trickle down the side), then make a shallow dip in the middle of the flour and add the yeast.
- Fit the pan into the bread machine, shut the lid and set to the basic white setting with a crust of your choice. Press start.
- After baking, lift the pan out of the machine using oven gloves. Carefully shake out the loaf to remove it from the pan, then transfer to a wire rack, standing the loaf on its base. Leave to cool.

Baker's tip
- Spelt bread is higher in protein than ordinary wheat bread. Bread made with spelt flour rises much more quickly than conventional wheat breads so should be cooked on the basic white rather than wholewheat bread machine setting.

Soft White Spelt Bread

This bread can often be enjoyed by those who find other wheat flours difficult to digest. The creamy coloured flour makes a pale brown loaf with a deliciously nutty flavour. This is a very simple loaf, but you could add some chopped nuts or seeds to the mixture if you like.

- Lift the bread pan out of the bread machine and fit the kneading blade. Pour the water into the bread pan. Add the oil, followed by the flour.
- Put the salt and sugar in separate corners of the pan, then make a shallow dip in the middle of the flour and add the yeast.
- Fit the pan into the bread machine, shut the lid and set to the basic white setting with a crust of your choice. Press start.
- Just as the baking cycle starts, sprinkle 1 tsp flour over the top through a sieve.
- After baking, lift the pan out of the machine using oven gloves. Carefully shake out the loaf to remove it from the pan, then transfer to a wire rack, standing the loaf on its base. Leave to cool.

Baker's tip
- If you forget to dust the top with flour before baking, dust the top after turning out of the bread pan, while the loaf is still hot.

Ingredients:
350ml water
2 tbsp sunflower oil
500g white spelt flour plus 1 tsp
1 tsp salt
1 tbsp soft light brown sugar
1¼ tsp fast-action dried yeast

Quantities for a large (900g) loaf
425ml water
2 tbsp sunflower oil
600g white spelt flour
1¼ tsp salt
4 tsp soft light brown sugar
1¼ tsp fast-action dried yeast

Quantities for a small (450g) loaf
215ml water
1 tbsp sunflower oil
300g white spelt flour
¾ tsp salt
2 tsp soft light brown sugar
¾ tsp fast-action dried yeast

Simple Gluten-free Bread

Ingredients:
300ml lukewarm water
2 medium eggs, lightly
    beaten
2 tsp lemon juice
3 tbsp sunflower oil
450g gluten-free white
    bread flour with added
    natural gum
1 tsp salt
1 tbsp caster sugar
2 tsp fast-action dried yeast

Quantities for a small (375g)
    loaf (suitable for compact
    models)
150ml lukewarm water
1 medium egg
1 tsp lemon juice
1½ tbsp sunflower oil
225g gluten-free white
    bread flour
½ tsp salt
1½ tsp caster sugar
1 tsp fast-action dried yeast

This loaf and is ideal for those who can't tolerate wheat or gluten. Make sure you buy gluten-free bread flour with added natural gum, as this gives a lighter bread with a more open texture. You can use white wine vinegar instead of lemon juice, if you prefer.

- Lift the bread pan out of the bread machine and fit the kneading blade. Pour the water, beaten eggs and lemon juice into the bread pan. Add the oil.
- Add the flour and put the salt and sugar in separate corners of the bread pan. Make a small hollow in the middle of the flour and add the yeast.
- Fit the pan into the bread machine, shut the lid and set to the gluten-free, rapid setting with a crust of your choice.
- After baking, lift the pan out of the machine using oven gloves. Carefully shake out the loaf to remove it from the pan, then transfer to a wire rack, standing the loaf on its base. Leave to cool.

Baker's tips
- If you have gluten-free bread flour without natural gum, add 1 tbsp of xanthum gum.
- This is not suitable for making as a larger loaf.
- Gluten-free loaves usually have flat, slightly bumpy tops, rather than a smooth dome.

Makes a 750g loaf

Gluten-free Brown Bread

Another recipe suitable for those avoiding wheat or gluten, balsamic vinegar adds depth to the flavour and colour, but you can use 1 tsp red or white wine vinegar and 1 tsp extra water if you prefer. Try adding a few toasted seeds or nuts or extra flavour and texture.

- Lift the bread pan out of the bread machine and fit the kneading blade. Pour the water into the bread pan. Add the beaten eggs and vinegar, then the oil. Add the flour.
- Put the salt and sugar in separate corners of the bread pan. Make a small hollow in the middle of the flour and add the yeast.
- Fit the pan into the bread machine, shut the lid and set to the gluten-free, rapid setting with a crust of your choice.
- After baking, lift the pan out of the machine using oven gloves. Carefully shake out the loaf to remove it from the pan, then transfer to a wire rack, standing the loaf on its base. Leave to cool.

Baker's tips
- If you have gluten-free bread flour without natural gum, add 1 tbsp of xanthum gum.
- This is not suitable for making as a larger loaf.

Ingredients:
300ml lukewarm water
2 tsp balsamic vinegar
2 medium eggs, lightly beaten
4 tbsp sunflower oil
400g gluten-free brown bread flour with added natural gum
1 tsp salt
2 tbsp soft light brown sugar
2 tsp fast-action dried yeast

Quantities for a small (375g) loaf
150ml lukewarm water
1 tsp balsamic vinegar
1 medium egg
2 tbsp sunflower oil
200g gluten-free brown bread flour with added natural gum
½ tsp salt
1 tbsp soft light brown sugar
1 tsp fast-action dried yeast

Gluten-free Cheese and Sun-dried Tomato Loaf

Ingredients:
200g wheat- and gluten-free plain white flour
¼ tsp salt (optional)
1 tbsp gluten-free baking powder
2 tsp tomato purée
2 tbsp olive oil
3 eggs
284ml buttermilk
50g sun-dried tomatoes in oil, coarsely chopped
40g Parmesan, finely grated

This is a wheat- and gluten-free loaf made without yeast and cooked on the bake setting. It has a lovely flavour provided by a combination of grated Parmesan and soft sun-dried tomatoes in oil, both of which are fairly salty, so don't be tempted to add extra salt.

- Lightly grease and line the bread pan with baking parchment, if specified in the manual.
- Put the flour, salt (if using) and baking powder in a mixing bowl and stir everything together. Make a hollow in the middle.
- Blend the tomato purée with a spoonful of the oil, then mix in the rest of the oil. Add the eggs and whisk with a fork, then stir in the buttermilk. Pour into the hollow, add the sun-dried tomatoes and about two-thirds of the Parmesan and mix together until blended.
- Spoon into the bread pan and sprinkle the top with the remaining Parmesan. Fit the pan into the breadmaker and set to the bake only programme. Select 50 minutes on the timer and choose a light crust (if this option is available). Press start.
- Check that the bread is cooked by gently pressing the surface with your fingers; it should feel firm. If necessary, re-set the timer and cook for a few more minutes.
- Remove the pan from the machine and leave to stand for 5 minutes, then carefully turn out on to a wire rack and leave to cool.

Baker's tips
- Instead of the olive oil, you could use a couple of spoonfuls of oil from the sun-dried tomatoes.
- If you can't find buttermilk, use the same amount of skimmed or semi-skimmed milk and stir in 2 tsp of lemon or lime juice. Leave for a few minutes before using.
- This is not suitable for making as a larger loaf.

Vegan Loaf

Vegans don't eat meat or fish or any products derived from them, including cow's milk, eggs and honey. While many of the recipes in this book are suitable or can simply be adapted, this bread contains a number of nutrients which may be lacking in a vegan diet.

- Lift the bread pan out of the bread machine and fit the kneading blade. Pour in the soya milk and add the oil. Add the wholemeal bread flour, followed by the milled flax and seed mix, then add the white bread flour.
- Put the salt and sugar in separate corners of the pan. Then make a shallow dip in the middle of the flour and add the yeast.
- Fit the pan into the bread machine, shut the lid and set to the basic white setting with a crust of your choice. Press start.
- After baking, lift the pan out of the machine using oven gloves. Carefully shake out the loaf to remove it from the pan, then transfer to a wire rack, standing the loaf on its base. Leave to cool.

Baker's tips
- If you can't find milled flax, sunflower, pumpkin and sesame seeds and goji berries mix, substitute 1 tbsp sesame seeds and 1 tbsp sunflower or pumpkin seeds instead.
- Vegan diets often lack vitamins B_{12} and D, calcium, iodine and omega 3. Choose a fortified soya milk when making this bread (containing additional B_{12}, vitamin D and calcium). Flaxseed and rapeseed oil are both a great source of omega 3 for vegans.
- This is not suitable for making as a larger loaf.

Ingredients:
325ml soya milk
2 tbsp rapeseed oil
250g strong wholemeal bread flour
2 tbsp milled flax, sunflower, pumpkin and sesame seeds and goji berries mix
250g strong white bread flour
1¼ tsp iodised salt
1 tbsp soft light brown sugar
1½ tsp fast-action dried yeast

Quantities for a small (450g) loaf
195ml soya milk
4 tsp rapeseed oil
150g strong wholemeal bread flour
4 tsp milled flax and seed mix
150g strong white bread flour
¾ tsp iodised salt
2 tsp soft light brown sugar
¾ tsp fast-action dried yeast

Cakes and Teabreads

Most bread machines can do much more than just bake bread or make bread dough ready for shaping and baking. Many also have a cake or baking programme enabling you to create some delicious treats. These traditional cakes and teabreads use baking powder as a raising agent instead of yeast and have moist even textures. On some machines, a cake programme will both mix and bake your cake; you simply have to add the ingredients. Others have a bake only programme where you will need to make the cake mixture as you would conventionally, then use the bread machine as a mini oven. For these, the mixing blade is removed and the base of the bread pan lined with baking parchment; you'll have to make a small hole in the middle to allow for the shaft. The resulting cake will be the same shape as a loaf of bread but much smaller; about 8cm high.

Refer to the manufacturer's guidelines when using this setting as some machines cook cakes a lot more quickly than others. In some machines the element is close to the pan and the sides of the cake can become quite brown before the cake is cooked. When baking cakes for the first time, test to see if it is ready about 10 minutes before the end of cooking time suggested in these recipes, so that you can adjust them next time, if necessary.

CHAPTER 10

Banana and Cinnamon Teabread

Ingredients:
100g butter
75 g light soft brown sugar
175g golden syrup
3 medium very ripe bananas
2 medium eggs
5 tbsp soured cream or thick natural yoghurt
5 tbsp milk
300g self-raising flour
1 tsp bicarbonate of soda
2 tsp ground cinnamon
Pinch of salt
50g chopped walnuts or pecans (optional)

This is a great way to use up ripe bananas which have been sitting in the fruit bowl too long. Quick and easy to prepare, this cut-and-come again cake makes a great snack or handy addition to lunchboxes.

- Lightly grease and line the bread pan with baking parchment, if specified in the manual.
- Put the butter, sugar and syrup in a small saucepan and gently heat until the butter has melted. Stir and leave to cool for a few minutes.
- Meanwhile, peel and mash the bananas in a bowl with a fork. Crack in the eggs and beat with the fork until mixed. Stir in the soured cream or yoghurt and the milk. Add the melted mixture and stir well.
- Sift over the flour, bicarbonate of soda, cinnamon and salt. Stir everything together until smooth (don't worry if there are a few lumps of banana), then spoon into the bread pan, smoothing the top level. Scatter the chopped nuts over the top, if using.
- Fit the pan into the breadmaker and set to the bake only programme. Select 1 hour 10 minutes on the timer. Press start.
- After baking, check that the cake is cooked by gently pressing the surface with your fingers; it should feel firm. If necessary, re-set the timer and cook for a few more minutes.
- Remove the pan from the machine and leave to stand for 5 minutes, then carefully turn out on to a wire rack and leave to cool.

Baker's tip
- Don't use the cake setting; this teabread is best mixed by hand and cooked on the bake only programme.

Tropical Fruit Teabread

Choose ready-to-eat exotic or tropical dried fruit for this tasty teabread. These come in mixed packets; the papaya, pineapple, mango and melon is a really colourful combination and works well here.

Ingredients:
75g butter
2 eggs
175ml milk
275g self-raising flour
Pinch of salt
125g caster sugar
25g desiccated coconut
100g ready-to-eat dried
   tropical fruits, chopped

- Lightly grease and line the bread pan with baking parchment, if specified in the manual.
- Put the butter in a small saucepan and heat gently until melted.
- Whisk the eggs in a large bowl with a fork, then add the milk and stir together. Pour in the melted butter. Sift over the flour, salt and caster sugar. Add the coconut and tropical fruits and gently fold everything together.
- Spoon into the bread pan, smoothing the top level. Fit the pan into the breadmaker and set to the bake only programme. Select 50 minutes on the timer. Press start.
- Check that the cake is cooked by gently pressing the surface with your fingers; it should feel firm. If necessary, re-set the timer and cook for a few more minutes.
- Remove the pan from the machine and leave to stand for 5 minutes, then carefully turn out on to a wire rack and leave to cool.

Baker's tips
- If your breadmaker has a cake programme, which mixes and bakes (rather than just baking), don't line the bread pan with baking parchment but fit the kneading blade. Pour the melted butter into the bread pan, then add the egg and milk mixture. Sift over the flour, salt and caster sugar, then add the coconut and tropical fruit. Select the cake programme and press start. After 6 minutes mixing, scrape down the sides with a plastic spatula to ensure all the ingredients are blended.
- To make a rum-flavoured frosting, sift 75g golden icing sugar into a bowl and stir in 3 tbsp rum until smooth and the consistency of thick pouring cream. Add a little more rum if needed. Spoon the icing over the teabread, letting it drizzle down the sides.

Moist and Sticky Gingerbread

Ingredients:

100g butter
100g light muscovado sugar
75g molasses or black
   treacle
200g golden syrup
50g stem ginger from a jar,
   finely chopped
225g self-raising flour
1 tsp ground mixed spice
1 tsp ground ginger
2 eggs
2 tbsp milk

This delicious ginger cake matures and becomes even stickier with keeping. After cooling, wrap in foil and keep somewhere cool for a few days before slicing and serving. You can leave out the chopped stem ginger, if you prefer.

- Lightly grease and line the bread pan with baking parchment, if specified in the manual.
- Put the butter in a large saucepan with the sugar, molasses or treacle, golden syrup and stem ginger. Gently heat until the butter has melted, stirring occasionally.
- Remove the pan from the heat, stir, then sift over the flour and spices. Stir until mixed together.
- Whisk the eggs and milk together. Add to the melted mixture and stir together until smooth.
- Pour the mixture into the bread pan. Fit the pan into the breadmaker and set to the bake only programme. Select 1 hour on the timer. Press start.
- Check that the cake is cooked by gently pressing the surface with your fingers; it should feel just firm. If necessary, re-set the timer and cook for a few more minutes.
- Remove the pan from the machine and leave to stand for 5 minutes, then carefully turn out on to a wire rack and leave to cool.

Baker's tip
- If your breadmaker has a cake programme, which mixes and bakes (rather than just baking), don't line the bread pan with baking parchment but fit the kneading blade. Pour the melted mixture into the bread pan, then add the egg and milk mixture. Sift over the flour and spices. Select the cake programme and press start. After 6 minutes mixing, scrape down the sides with a plastic spatula to ensure all the ingredients are blended.

Cuts into 8 slices

Frosted Carrot Cake

If you can't resist the temptation of a slice of really moist cake smothered in a creamy frosting, this is the perfect – and reasonably healthy – choice. You can of course, leave it without the icing if you prefer a plainer cake.

- Lightly grease the bread pan and line with baking parchment, if specified in the manual.
- Put the sugar and oil in a large mixing bowl and, using a wire whisk or electric hand-mixer on a low speed, whisk for a few minutes until blended and slightly lighter in colour.
- Add the eggs, one at a time, beating well between each addition. Sift over the flour, bicarbonate of soda, cinnamon, ginger and salt and start folding in. When half-mixed, add the walnuts, orange zest and juice and grated carrots, then continue mixing until combined.
- Pour the mixture into the bread pan. Fit the pan into the breadmaker and set to the bake only programme. Select 1 hour on the timer. Press start.
- Check that the cake is cooked by gently pressing the surface with your fingers; it should feel firm. If necessary, re-set the timer and cook for a few more minutes.
- Remove the pan from the machine and leave to stand for 5 minutes, then carefully turn out on to a wire rack and leave to cool.
- To make the frosting, sift the icing sugar into a bowl. Add the butter and beat together until smooth. Beat in the soft cheese, then the orange or lemon juice. Spread over the top of the cold cake.

Baker's tip
- This cake is best mixed by hand and cooked on the bake only programme, rather than using the cake option.

Ingredients:
175g light muscovado sugar
150ml sunflower oil
3 eggs
225g self-raising flour
1 tsp bicarbonate of soda
1½ tsp ground cinnamon
½ tsp ground ginger
Pinch of salt
75g chopped walnuts, preferably toasted
Finely grated zest of 1 orange
2 tbsp orange juice
200g finely grated carrot (2–3 carrots)

For the frosting
50g icing sugar
50g butter, softened
100g full-fat soft cheese, at room temperature
1 tsp orange or lemon juice

Rich Chocolate Cake

Ingredients:
125g butter, softened
75g soft light brown sugar
25g clear honey
2 eggs, lightly beaten
100g self-raising flour
25g cocoa powder
½ tsp baking powder
2 tsp milk
1 tsp vanilla extract
For the chocolate fudge
   frosting
150g plain chocolate, broken
   into pieces
75g butter
75g icing sugar

This dark chocolate cake, cooked in your breadmaker, surpasses any oven-baked version and is beautifully moist and even-textured. A fudgy chocolate frosting adds the final flourish or you can leave the cake plain and simply dust with a little icing sugar before serving.

- Lightly grease the bread pan and line with baking parchment, if specified in the manual.
- Put the butter, sugar and honey in a large mixing bowl and beat together until light and fluffy. Add the eggs, a little at a time, beating well between each addition. Sift over the flour, cocoa and baking powder and fold in with the milk and vanilla extract.
- Spoon and scrape the mixture into the bread pan and level the top. Fit the pan into the breadmaker and set to the bake only programme. Select 50 minutes on the timer. Press start.
- Check that the cake is cooked by gently pressing the surface with your fingers; it should feel firm. If necessary, re-set the timer and cook for a few more minutes.
- Remove the pan from the machine and leave to stand for 5 minutes, then carefully turn out on to a wire rack and leave to cool.
- For the frosting, break the chocolate into a heatproof bowl and add the butter. Place the bowl over a pan of near-boiling water and leave for a few minutes. Stir until melted, then remove the bowl. Sift the icing sugar into the bowl and stir until well-mixed. Spread over the top and sides of the cold cake and leave to set.

Baker's tip
- This cake is best mixed by hand and cooked on the bake only programme, rather than using the cake option.

Cuts into 8 slices

Oat and Blueberry Muffin Loaf

Like most muffins, this is easy to prepare and should be eaten while really fresh; preferably on the same day as making. Do soak the dried blueberries with the oat and milk mixture; it allows them to start soaking up some of the liquid, making them moist and juicy.

- Lightly grease the bread pan and line with baking parchment, if specified in the manual.
- Put the blueberries and oats in a large bowl and pour over the milk and vanilla extract. Stir, then set aside to soak for 10 minutes.
- Put the flour, baking powder, salt and sugar into a large bowl and stir to mix well. Stir the egg and oil into the oat mixture. Add the oat mixture to the dry ingredients and mix briefly until just combined. Spoon and scrape the mixture into the prepared bread pan.
- Fit the pan into the breadmaker and set to the bake only programme. Select 50 minutes on the timer and choose a light crust (if this selection is available). Press start.
- Check that the cake is cooked by gently pressing the surface with your fingers; it should feel springy. If necessary, re-set the timer and cook for a few more minutes.
- Remove the pan from the machine and leave to stand for 5 minutes, then carefully turn out on to a wire rack.
- When the cake is barely warm, blend the icing sugar and orange juice or water together to make a thin icing. Drizzle over the top of the cake. Serve warm or cold.

Baker's tip
- This cake is also delicious served hot or warm as a dessert with custard.

Ingredients:
- 100g packet dried blueberries
- 50g porridge oats
- 275ml milk
- 2 tsp vanilla extract
- 225g self-raising wholemeal flour
- 1 tsp baking powder
- ¼ tsp salt
- 150g soft light brown sugar
- 1 egg, lightly beaten
- 6 tbsp sunflower oil
- 40g icing sugar, sifted
- 2 tsp orange juice or water

Wholemeal Honey, Ginger and Lemon Tea Loaf

Ingredients:
1 lemon and ginger tea bag
225g plain wholemeal flour
1 tsp baking powder
1 tsp ground ginger
Pinch of salt
100g butter
50g caster sugar
100g walnut pieces
3 tbsp clear honey
2 eggs, lightly beaten

For the icing
50g icing sugar, sifted
25g walnut halves

Lemon and ginger tea has been used to ice this loaf, which is also delicately flavoured with the tea, honey and walnuts. Serve thickly sliced as a tea-time treat or mid-morning coffee break. Thinly spreading with a little soft creamy butter is an optional extra.

- Lightly grease the bread pan and line with baking parchment, if specified in the manual.
- Brew the lemon and ginger tea with 75ml boiling water. Allow to infuse for 6 minutes, then remove the teabag, squeezing out as much liquid as possible.
- Meanwhile, sift the flour, baking powder, ginger and salt into a bowl, adding the bran left in the sieve. Cut the butter into small pieces, add to the bowl and rub in until the mixture resembles fine breadcrumbs. Stir in the sugar and walnut pieces.
- Mix the honey, eggs and 2 tbsp of the tea together in a jug, add to the dry mixture and gently mix together. Spoon and scrape the mixture into the prepared bread pan.
- Fit the pan into the breadmaker and set to the bake only programme. Select 50 minutes on the timer and choose a light crust (if this selection is available). Press start.
- Check that the cake is cooked by gently pressing the surface with your fingers; it should feel springy. If necessary, re-set the timer and cook for a few more minutes.
- Remove the pan from the machine and leave to stand for 5 minutes, then carefully turn out on to a wire rack. Leave to cool.
- To make the icing, stir 1–2 tbsp of the remaining tea into the icing sugar to make a fairly thick icing. Drizzle over the top of the cake and decorate with walnut halves. Leave to set before serving.

Baker's tip
- For a change, make the loaf with orange-flavoured tea, maple syrup and pecans.

Cuts into 8 slices

Gluten-free Citrus Cake

Although mashed potato may sound a surprising ingredient, it makes a deliciously moist and light cake and many tasters won't believe it's there! This sponge is flavoured with both orange and lemon zest and drizzled with a sticky lemon syrup after baking.

- Lightly grease the bread pan and line with baking parchment, if specified in the manual.
- Put the butter, sugar and salt in a large mixing bowl and beat together until light and fluffy. Add the eggs, a little at a time, beating well between each addition.
- Beat in the polenta, then fold in the mashed potato, lemon and lime zest and baking powder.
- Spoon and scrape the mixture into the bread pan and level the top. Fit the pan into the breadmaker and set to the bake only programme. Select 1 hour on the timer. Press start.
- Check that the cake is cooked by gently pressing the surface with your fingers; it should feel firm. If necessary, re-set the timer and cook for a few more minutes.
- Remove the pan from the machine and leave to stand for 5 minutes, then carefully turn out on to a wire rack.
- Stir the granulated sugar and lemon and lime juice together until some of the sugar has dissolved. Spoon over the hot cake. Leave the cake to cool.

Baker's tip
- Use potatoes that have been mashed without added butter, milk or seasonings.

Ingredients:
100g butter, softened
150g golden caster sugar
Pinch of salt
3 eggs
130g polenta
200g cold mashed potato, at room temperature
Finely grated zest of 1 small lemon
Finely grated zest of 1 lime
2 tsp gluten-free baking powder

For the drizzle
6 tbsp granulated sugar
Juice of 1 small lemon
Juice of 1 lime

Index